SOLATULIP

SOLATULIP

Poems and meditations on the Five Solas and T.U.L.I.P.

P. D. Gray

RESOURCE *Publications* · Eugene, Oregon

SOLATULIP
Poems and meditations on the Five Solas and T.U.L.I.P.

Resource Publications
An Imprint of Wipf and Stock Publishers
199 W. 8th Ave., Suite 3
Eugene, OR 97401

www.wipfandstock.com

PAPERBACK ISBN: 978-1-7252-8380-0
HARDCOVER ISBN: 978-1-7252-8373-2
EBOOK ISBN: 978-1-7252-8376-3

Let the word of Christ dwell in you richly in all wisdom; teaching and admonishing one another in psalms and hymns and spiritual songs, singing with grace in your hearts to the Lord (Colossians 3:16).

Dedications

I would particularly like to thank Mr Burrows and Pastor Byrd for their kind words of encouragement, as I labor in a task which is so unpopular and unpalatable to many. Who, after all, craves poetry and meditations in our day and age, let alone Christian poetry and meditations! Nevertheless, much of the Bible is poetic and meditative in nature, and I find myself a mere scratcher at the surface of Scripture as I try to express myself in a way which is in tune with it and, I hope, reverent.

I am also very thankful for the fellowship and godly counsel of my brothers in Christ, the aptly named Sola, and Lincoln. Their conversations have sharpened my own understanding; their warmth and sincerity have often humbled me.

May the Lord use these musings to draw souls to cherish the Scriptures even more, day by day, until that final day shall come when we will have no more need of faith or hope, for we shall know even as we are known.

Contents

Author's note

During a period in the journey of our family in which we were away from sound, Reformed Christian teaching for a season, I started to question what the *essence* of the Christian faith really is. I started to reflect upon that which is essential to Christianity and realized that it isn't primarily to do with denomination, fellowship, outreach, hymnody, worship style, dress code, heritage, although these things are certainly important and under satanic attack like never before. Ultimately, though, true Christianity has to do with the knowledge of God and the knowledge of self, insofar as we can comprehend these things in our mortal condition.

"My people are destroyed for a lack of knowledge . . ." God tells us in His word, and this can apply both in terms of initial conversion and subsequent sanctification. The more we seek to know God and self, the more love we will have for the holy and spiritual, the less inclined to think and act foolishly according to the world's prioritizing of health, wealth, money, power, pleasure, status etc. When a truly converted Christian finds his or her soul growing cold to the things of God, manifests *less* zeal for the things of God, *less* communion in private and *less* congregating in public, it is likely that it is these essential moorings which have been lost sight of, not sufficiently clung to, not adequately thought about, not sincerely loved.

These truths do not necessarily instruct us with regard to the practical outworking of the Christian life; for that, we are to turn to the glorious Sermon on the Mount. However, before we get to that blessed Sermon of sermons, we should deepen our knowledge of the principles of Christianity, the essence of what it means for a sinful, wretched creature to approach the Almighty Creator and the truth of how this came about, ie. from self or from God, or from both? When we begin to hold these wonderful things in view, then and only then are we ready to ascend that blessed mountain of Matthew 5 and feel something of the weight of those awe-ful, holy verses. It is crucial to get this the right way round, lest we fall into the trap of thinking we can somehow deserve or improve upon God's sovereign investment in us. We cannot.

The Five Solas, then, came into sharper relief during that momentous time known as the Reformation. After the burning zeal and godly-mindedness of the first three centuries of Christianity, spanning parts of the Middle-East, the then world HQ—Rome, and some of that vast continent of Africa, the seeds of decline came at that point when the kingdom of this world decided to try and wed itself to the kingdom of God; the former was greatly blessed and ennobled while the latter greatly diluted and impoverished, spiritually speaking. We learn from the Bible's first four chapters that these two kingdoms are perpetually at war, one with the other, never the twain meeting in the true sense. The Five Solas arose, therefore, as five banners of 'protest' against centuries of compromise, obfuscation, mysticism and willful ignorance of the holy Scriptures.

Sola Scriptura (Scripture alone) brings us back to the ultimate authority for all things. The authority for claiming to know God and self rests not on the shoulders of any wise man or ongoing scientific proof, but within the God-breathed pages of 66 books penned by around 40 human instruments in various places, over a millennium and a half. No human can be accredited with it, while all knowledge which is saving and worthwhile is to be found within it; it has given rise to and yet infinitely transcends all tradition, hymnody, sermonizing, catechisms, confessions, poetry, meditations, philosophy, systematic theologies, creeds, customs, treatises under the sun. Only the Bible is our final authority, despite these afore-mentioned means being great helps and guides, having illuminated many parts of this transcendent, divinely arranged library. Nobody, however, has fully comprehended or satisfactorily plumbed the infinite depths of holy Scripture. It is its own best interpreter and explainer and will reward those who honor it, resort to it, rest upon it as their final authority.

Sola Fide (Faith alone) stands in stark contrast with *plus* anything, be it good works, church government, church fellowship, societal outreach, global missions, universities, schools, hospitals, governments, or anything else in which humans trust and abide. Such things have been enormously benefited and inspired by the influence of Christianity over the centuries (read Mr Burrows' 'Our Priceless Christian Heritage' 2020), but it is only by *faith* that any soul who has ever walked may please God. Faith is the abandonment of human works in terms of misusing them to promote self. Faith can contain not one particle of human merit, otherwise it ceases to be faith, becoming its enemy. Saving faith is therefore a departure from trust in human ability or power. It is contrary to the normal course of human endeavor in which we seek to empower self, viewing it as sufficient.

Sola Gratia (Grace alone) reminds us of our enormous mountain of pride which would seek to gain the mastery over our lives, if it could. The fact is, we would soon start to take pride in our faith if we were not reminded in God's word that our faith is God-given; it was by God's grace we came to have and to hold it. Because it *was* graciously given, we can therefore take no pride in it or claim any merit for having had it and continuing to have it. It is true that believers are described as having stronger faith over time, sometimes viewed as being of relatively stronger or weaker faith when compared with each other. But the truth is, without grace no one would have faith—faith is not produced from within but received only by grace.

Solo Christo (In Christ alone) has sometimes been *Solus Christus*, which means *Only Christ*. Both are equally true, although my preference for the purpose of this book is for this *Solo* grammatical construction because it reminds us that our journey to our ultimate destination (*Solus Christus*) is not made by us acting autonomously or improving upon the initial work that God has begun within us, but is very much in and through Christ (*Solo Christo*) every step of the way. He is, of course, 'the way, the truth, and the life'—we stand before God *in* Christ, move towards God *through* Christ, eventually to enter the very presence *of* Christ when we have shuffled off this mortal coil and exist immortally.

Soli Deo Gloria (Glory to God alone) is the statement and state of being in which we will be dwelling forever, thus it defines and overwhelms us because we are currently existing in a place of sin, time, death. When we get an amazing benefit or reward on earth, *Soli Deo Gloria*. When we suffer a terrible illness or setback, *Soli Deo Gloria*. If our personal enemy and antagonist ends up in heaven, *Soli Deo Gloria*. If our closest loved one ends up in hell, *Soli Deo Gloria*. Truly the thoughts of God are not our thoughts, our ways are not His ways. If we seek to turn ourselves over to God and remember this final *sola* in particular, we are well on the way to achieving that most precious and rare jewel—Christian contentment.

The second set of truths came about a little later on, once the Reformation had arisen and begun to radiate renewed light into the world. Throughout every peak there comes a trough; with every victory a satanic counterfeit. So it was in those generations post Reformation, ergo the need for those so-called Doctrines of Grace, sometimes called Calvinism, sometimes T.U.L.I.P. to robustly put up a defense against that which would try to subvert and pervert God's rekindling of His Word.

Total Depravity, rightly understood, does not mean that every human is depraved in the commonly understood tabloid newspaper term. Nor does it mean that we are all as bad as we could be, for then earth and hell would be indistinguishable. It really points out that every one of us shares a common humanity—fallen, incapable of existing without sin, subject to death, facing judgement. It is a bit like biting into an apple only to discover it is riddled with putrefaction. There may be good bits therein, but the thing is incapable of pleasing and so is fit for throwing away. Our original, corrupted human nature, whether as bad as or better than our neighbor's is not fit for purpose we are; utterly unfit for heaven. This bad news must be faced up to if we are properly to desire the good news.

Unconditional Election is, regrettably, sometimes seen as something only for the mature Christian or Bible scholar. This should not be, for it enlarges the mind of a regular Christian and humbles a worldly reader of the Bible to the dust, DV, helping them to see upon what basis they too might become a believer.. Just as we cannot claim that our physical birth originated in our personal decision or choice (we didn't one day decide to ask our earthly parents to conceive us), so too our spiritual birth cannot ultimately be attributed to a day of decision or moment of surrender. It was in eternity when such a thing was conceived, which completely strips us of any form of pride and self-determination. It should not deter a regular, worldly human from seeking after salvation, because the free offer of the Gospel is held out in so many places and in so many ways, throughout Scripture. Even creation itself hints at it with its light coming after darkness, spring after winter and so on.

Limited Atonement is probably the most contested and unpopular doctrine in the Bible-believing churches of our day. Perhaps the word 'limited' is unfortunate; *particular* or *specific* might help some to get a better grasp of it. God, who likens Himself to a potter in both Testaments, did not embark upon the process of saving millions of souls without sufficient foresight and preparation. It was His plan from eternity to redeem vast multitudes of specific sinners from all corners of the globe, throughout every era of time. Just as there will be an ordained multitude in heaven, so there will be an ordained multitude in hell. Whether there will be more in one than the other is not known by us (although if every aborted baby ends up in heaven then it would seem to tilt the balance in heaven's favor). If we have any sincere, saving interest in God, the cause of this must be traced into eternity, outside of this realm of time.

Irresistible Grace explains why it was that, in such and such a place and in such and such a time we found ourselves coming to know and to love the Lord. It magnifies the glorious role of the Holy Spirit in inclining our minds and hearts to our Father in heaven. The Holy Spirit will never forcefully overwhelm or strong-arm a soul into heavenly mindedness, but will gently illuminate the mind and regenerate the soul so that it is enabled to see the light. The prodigal son, a prime example, is described as having come to himself, showing how we become a truer, more complete version of our selves the moment we are converted or born from above. We never would have come to ourselves were it not for God taking the initiative and graciously drawing us.

Perseverance of the Saints is a warning to those who would abuse the privilege of grace, claiming 'once saved always saved' to live loosely, in practice adding a sixth, counterfeit *Sola—Gloria Sui Solum* (Glory to self alone). I emphasize 'in practice' for in theory so many presumptuous Christians, like the golden-calf worshippers of Moses' day, falsely believe they *are* glorifying God when in fact they are not. The believer will therefore be tested throughout life's journey; some in one way, some in another. The true believer will persevere, will overcome, perhaps losing battles but winning in the end because the war has already been won by our Conqueror. Through Him we are superior to worldly conquerors who only apprehend material goods and earthly property.

By assembling these ten essential truths of Christianity in close proximity, concentrating them, my hope is that they will remind us to step back for a moment and meditate a little more on God's glory, claiming not one iota of credit for our initial conversion, nor our long and winding pilgrimage. It may be that you have been backsliding somewhat in recent months or have become downcast, feeling the weight of the world upon your shoulders. It could even be that you have shied away from the middle 'L' of T.U.L.I.P, not wanting to consider the dire consequences of rejecting it, shown in John 6:66.

Whatever the case may be, may the great and infinite, all-knowing God be pleased to bless our minds, that we may walk with Him.

Sola scriptura 1

Those who "add unto" or "take away from" the Word of God are condemned by it in the strongest of terms (Rev 22:18-19, also Deut 4:2, 12:32). They are not only violating the 8th commandment but are blocking the path to the City of Refuge, the holy Kingdom of Christ. I remember listening to a Christian radio presenter–preacher for a number of years, but never being saved until, according to God's providential will, I heard the Word of God being faithfully and fearlessly preached by another more biblically faithful pastor.

The greatest care should be taken when handling the Word of God; it was, after all, a godly man, Aaron, who foolishly facilitated false worship via "a molten calf" (Exod 32:4). As *they* brought in something else alongside true worship, are *we* not in danger the moment we turn to a preacher, denomination, Bible version, commentary, or any other means which may subtly start to rival or supplant the inerrant God-breathed Word in some way?

Dear heavenly Father, will I put my thoughts alongside Thy thoughts, my ways on a par with Thy ways (Isa 55:8)? Will I merely use my "eyes" (Gen 13:10) and reason with my common sense, or will I follow Thy Word to the cross of Christ, "the place of the altar" and call "on the name of the LORD" (Gen 13:4)? May such questions convict and return each of us to that never-failing, unquenchable, blessed Word, "lest that by any means, when I have preached to others, I myself should be a castaway" (1 Cor 9:27).

Verses referred to

Genesis 13:4, 10	Isaiah 55:8
Exodus 32:4	1 Corinthians 9:27
Deuteronomy 4:2, 12:32	Revelation 22:18—19

Bible reading

Oh steal not from your Bible reading
through it God your soul is leading,
worship not your commentary
nor hymnody nor poetry.

Oh steal not from your meditations
God's Word solves all situations,
tyrants are by words appeased
our Father by true hearts is pleased.

Oh steal not from daily devotions
harbor not your private notions,
holy men were moved of God
the Bible's author's none but God.

Oh steal not from the holy Scriptures
they're your life, not human strictures,
heaven, earth will pass away
the Word of God each soul will weigh.

Sola fide 1

Faith may be defined by the world as many things, but in biblical understanding it is that which is counter-intuitive to *flesh*. It is being born from above (John 3), the reversal of the inevitable consequences of the Fall (Gen 3). It is a looking unto Jesus and a rising up from one's impossible, sin-stained condition (Heb 12:1-3). It is a yielding and adhering to the eternal reality of things (2 Cor 4:18), an ongoing refuge from the nightmare of this world's deceitful system (v.4).

Faith is that which is most precious, most sought after by God, that which will become more scarce as the world rolls toward its pre-ordained conclusion: "I tell you that he will avenge them speedily. Nevertheless when the Son of man cometh, shall he find faith on the earth?" (Luke 18:8). Faith is something we want more of: "And the apostles said unto the Lord, Increase our faith" (17:5), and yet are counselled not to seek quality over quantity: "And the Lord said, If ye had faith as a grain of mustard seed, ye might say unto this sycamine tree, Be thou plucked up by the root, and be thou planted in the sea; and it should obey you" (v.6).

Faith must be exercised, or it is not true faith but counterfeit faith: "Even so faith, if it hath not works, is dead, being alone" (Jas 2:17). May we seek sincerely to apply faith to our bigger picture desires and decisions as well as to the minutiae of daily existence; not one without the other. Surely there is nothing too big nor too small that prayer cannot encompass, honoring the God in whom all our single lines of faith together are tethered.

Verses referred to

Genesis 3	2 Corinthians 4:4, 18
Luke 17:5—6, 18:8	Hebrews 12:1—3
John 3	James 2:17

Even you

Think not upon an unclean thought
for you're the slave whom God has bought,
but if you do, don't bury it
confess, don't play the hypocrite.

Relinquish every selfish plan
remember you are but a man,
God gave you every minute's breath
Christ is your hope, approaching death.

Forsake the world within your heart
stay in it, witness, don't depart,
a monk remains within his cell
the saved preach Christ who warned of hell.

Put all your faith in God the Son
all things are second, He is One,
remember God's free gift to you
you gave God nothing, even you.

Sola gratia 1

If faith is the fuel, then grace is the vehicle whereby a sinner is saved, for "by grace are ye saved through faith; and that not of yourselves: *it is* the gift of God" (Eph 2:8). The Holy Spirit is emphasizing how even our faith can swell us up and fuel our pride, hence the need to show how the whole project, plan, *vehicle* of man's salvation is of the Lord, or it is not salvation. We are but passengers and although from our human perspective designers and/or drivers of the vehicle, see with grace-filled eyes that "we are his workmanship" (v. 10), created and put into the vehicle in the first place (in fact Christ Jesus is designer, driver, and destination).

Alarmingly, "until the day dawn, and the day star arise in your hearts" (2 Pet 1:19) you were trapped in a demonic car factory, either proudly overestimating the control you thought was yours, or underestimating it, becoming a fatalistic crash-test dummy. Without grace you cannot let go, cannot trust in God to save "to the uttermost" (Heb 7:25), both in terms of the depth of original sin and longevity of it (can God pardon *all* of my sins until the end of my earthly journey, even after being saved!?)

We see this struggle throughout the tortuous dialogue of Job and his outward friends. We witness the struggle of our own souls, surrounded by ungracious, grace-doubting voices (even our own internal voices). Personally, I know that when I was born again I was all too ready to accept the deep and overwhelming need for grace; but am I equally ready to accept this necessity along life's road? May God enable us to persevere to the uttermost, for we are indeed being saved *sola gratia* today with the same grace with which we were saved all those miles ago: "Whereunto I also labour, striving according to his working, which worketh in me mightily" (Col 1:29).

Verses referred to

Ephesians 2:8, 10

Colossians 1:29

Hebrews 7:25

2 Peter 1:19

The gift

A gift simply cannot be earned
it's that which someone gives to you,
man's will by nature won't be turned
God has to shine the Son in you.

God's grace of course is undeserved
man tries in vain to pay for it,
it's full forgiveness, undeserved
for grace cannot contain merit.

A gift by default's not the giver,
he who was the cause of it,
to love the gift and not the giver
makes the gift a counterfeit.

God's grace is seldom understood
man tries to make it down to you,
though man makes with, but made not wood
wood's Maker died on wood, for you.

Solo Christo 1

Worship of Mary is arguably foreshadowed in the book of Jeremiah: "But we will certainly do whatsoever thing goeth forth out of our own mouth, to burn incense unto the queen of heaven . . ." (44:17). When man's feelings and mystical inclinations take the lead, there is no limit to the distortions and corruptions that can be made of God's infallible, unchangeable word. Having grown up attending a Roman Catholic church I know first-hand the extent to which it thrives upon a mysterious, unattainable form of experiential ignorance.

Whenever we exalt a created man or woman or angel we are in trouble, and need to be warned as in Iconium, "Sirs, why do ye these things?" (Acts 14:15) or Patmos, "See *thou do it* not" (Rev 22:9). That is not to say that Roman Catholicism is the sole cause of evil in the long history of the church, for the later wars of Reformation in Europe and persecution of sincere believers who didn't subscribe to the sacral society of the day, go to show that religious "man is born to trouble, as the sparks fly upwards" (Job 5:7).

As we scrutinize the Bible let us approach it reverently, being wary of the numerous intellectual minds which have gone astray by stepping outside of or trampling upon its hallowed ground, being "corrupted from the simplicity that is in Christ" (2 Cor 11:3). For that matter let us not be those who in our pride say we love Christ but do not love His unworldly, uncelebrated servants who solemnly preach His word each Lord's Day; for "He that receiveth whomsoever I send receiveth me" (John 13:20). If we love Christ we will love His ministers who expound His word.

Verses referred to

Job 5:7	Acts 14:15
Jeremiah 44:17	2 Corinthians 11:3
John 13:20	Revelation 22:9

Anno Domini

From Father God to mother church
our false, unholy lives did lurch,
from hail Caesar to hail Mary
we put a price on Christ, a fee.

From frankincense to innocence
we fell for worldly confidence,
from rosary's nativity
we hid within activity.

From sinful yeast to holy priest
we said that John was more than least,
from forcing folk to celibacy
Paul alone—our legacy.

From focusing upon our pope
we held up Peter as our hope.
from playing penitential games,
we misled people, misread James . . .

From crusades and inquisitions
you betrayed your own traditions,
from your putting down of Bible
we of God became your rival.

From the blood which then was spilled
we mixed the message God has willed,
that Jesus Christ's the whole, the Way,
through Him alone we are to pray.

Soli Deo Gloria 1

Unlike the many mocking depictions of the Bible or even the presumptuous art of a Michelangelo, actual biblical encounters with God have led to speechlessness, followed by a humble and heartfelt outpouring of praise. We think of Moses who "hid his face; for he was afraid to look upon God" (Exod 3:6), or Nebuchadnezzar who after being restored from a bestial dumbness immediately "blessed" then "praised and honoured him that liveth for ever" (Dan 4:34).

Beyond even these experiences is the supreme mystery of the incarnation of God; the One through whom came all things "that are in heaven, and that are in earth, visible and invisible" (Col 1:16), allowing Himself to become as one of us, "heard", "seen", "looked upon", "handled" (1 John 1:1). The limited, fallen mind cannot compute; it is too great even for the redeemed, enlightened mind to fully comprehend.

Nevertheless, there will come a time when we *will* understand it, as fully as it is possible for our created frames to bear; a time when we will be "clothed upon, that mortality might be swallowed up of life" (2 Cor 5:4). In that time we will have "no need of the sun, neither of the moon, to shine . . . for the glory of God" will "lighten . . . and the Lamb" will be "the light thereof" (Rev 21:23).

Toppled, all false gods of logic,

these things are discerned by faith.

Verses referred to

Exodus 3:6	Colossians 1:16
Daniel 4:34	1 John 1:1
2 Corinthians 5:4	Revelation 21:23

New heaven

Thou dwellest in eternal glory
far beyond our temporal story,
infinite, no valley, peak
so holy, creatures cannot speak.

Thou livest in transcendent glory
far beyond our highest storey,
over all, Thou seest all
before time was—those ones Thou'dst call.

Thou camest from heaven to earth
the Son incarnate, human girth,
the Father, Spirit, up above
the angels lost in chords of love.

Thou lovest man as God the Son
though one day Thou wilt take the sun,
this starry blanket will enfold
new heaven—souls bodies behold.

Total depravity 1

The concept of total depravity is, of course, shocking. We like to think that there are redeeming features in all people, and to a certain extent there are. However, the iceberg lies much deeper than we can see; we are dealing with a God who is utterly higher and holier than any mind can comprehend, and we depend entirely upon Divine revelation to know a) about our Creator, b) about ourselves.

Abraham, despite knowing something of his own total depravity ("dust and ashes" Gen 18:27) struggled to accept the total depravity of the inhabitants of Sodom and Gomorrah ("Peradventure ten shall be found there." v. 32), each city being just a Sydney or San Francisco of its day, until that solemn day of judgement. More shocking still is the extent to which sin can ruin not just the worldly but the nominally religious, if not rooted in Christ eg. Lot's wife.

The religious folk of Christ's days in the flesh could not see the irony of "I came not to call the righteous, but sinners to repentance" (Mark 2:17), blind to the fact that there are no righteous people outside of Christ. Moreover, Paul reasoned with the religious Galatians whom he deeply loved, "Are ye so foolish? having begun in the Spirit, are ye now made perfect by the flesh?" (Gal 3:3). Evidently many of them could not at that stage see the extent to which, in and of themselves, they were no good, id est, the flesh can do nothing spiritual.

As you and I struggle with our noxious, in-dwelling weeds, as we strive earnestly for the fruit of the Holy Spirit, may we better grasp that blessèd ladder between us and the Almighty: "For *there is* one God, and one mediator between God and men, the man Christ Jesus." (1 Tim 2:5). Let us put no faith in this world's Titanics, being found clinging simply to the Cross until we meet our Father—or Christ arrives in glory. The flesh in one sense can do many impressive things, but it cannot please God or enter heaven.

Verses referred to

Genesis 18:27, 32	Galatians 3:3
Mark 2:17	1 Timothy 2:5

He's my link

From somewhere very deep inside
comes foolish sin and stubborn pride,
oh it is more than to decide
it's Christ who in me must reside.

From somewhere very dark within
comes every anti-Christian sin,
it's not enough to turn from sin
if I do not with Christ begin.

From somewhere very bad in me
comes all the heartache I can see,
for only in Christ's purity
do I find peace and surety.

From somewhere very good I think
comes through the Word the fact I stink,
God sees the place where I do blink
I'm weak, I need Christ, He's my link.

Unconditional election 1

The "ye have not chosen me, but I have chosen you" (John 15:16) bombshell should resonate in the ears of every saved sinner throughout time's holy war. Indeed, the "no man can come unto me" (John 6:65) force-field was the thing which repelled "many of his disciples" (John 6:66), presumably false or mistaken ones. They simply could not cope with the fact that all the initiating glory, honor, and credit is in God and not in man (they apparently could not deal with having the truth so plainly spelt out—a valuable example for preachers in all ages to please God before man).

The "flesh" is certainly at war with the "Spirit" (Gal 5:17), actively seeking to subvert and discredit the word of God. If it could it would make salvation creditable to its own account, seeking to do all kinds of things to honor itself through a vast array of incentives and rewards. "By works" not "by grace" is its desperate desire, saved through self not "through faith" its unholy agenda; by the constantly evolving self not "the gift of God" does it weave its deadly ideology. Certainly "of works" is its mantra, and all so it can boast of its own achievements and abilities, minimizing to extinction the sovereignty of God; it is the *flesh's* grand anti-thesis to the powerful and life-changing thesis of Ephesians 2:8-9.

The woman of Samaria was treated with respect, questioned not just commanded, listened to as well as conversed with, drawn by grace to the point where she sincerely and earnestly cried out to the God-man, "Sir, give me this water, that I thirst not" (John 4:15). She was as each of us, an unlikely candidate, sought not seeking, approached while still an enemy, not wanting to regard herself in the same camp as "dogs, and sorcerers, and whoremongers, and murderers, and idolaters, and whosoever loveth and maketh a lie" (Rev 22:15).

And yet from eternity God purposed her to be purged "with hyssop", cleansed, washed and made "whiter than snow" (Ps 51:7). What human mind could devise such an unexpected and gracious plan? What philosophical, political, or religious system on earth exhibits such paternal admonition, such intimate and unconditional love? And where else can a soul turn, to find that fathomless well of spiritual, life-giving "waters" other than to Christ, to whom we may come "without money and without price" (Isa 55:1)?

Verses referred to

Psalm 51:7	Galatians 5:17
Isaiah 55:1	Ephesians 2:8—9
John 4:15, 6:65—66, 15:16	Revelation 22:15

Woman of Samaria

Oh woman of Samaria
you were a sick and thirsty soul,
the gossip of your area
without a moral aim or goal.

Oh woman you were immoral
husbands one, two, three, four and five,
you didn't even try to quarrel
knowing well your sin alive.

Oh woman, a Samaritan
despisèd people, not of God,
still chosen, oh Samaritan
before creation, known of God.

Oh woman you were confounded
and had to tell it straight away,
you spoke and they were astounded
your eyes opened, closed now to pray.

Limited atonement 1

Limited atonement is perhaps more helpfully thought of as specific or particular atonement, ie. unique to individuals who were created for the sole purpose of glorifying their Creator through the salvation of their souls. The normal, relatable nature of Christ's chosen disciples is a source of much comfort. We concur with Peter when he says "Depart from me; for I am a sinful man" (Luke 5:8). We too have felt our utter unworthiness in the presence of God the Spirit, and feel amazed that we have been brought to know Him.

Andrew, moreover, parallels our own sense of excitement: "We have found the Messias, which is, being interpreted, the Christ" (John 1:41). We admire his desire to reach out to his brother and not keep it to himself. We also find in his confession an echo of our own relief at having found not 'a' Christ but 'the' Christ; the One through whom all things were created, the only One through whom we may have hope.

We can test our faith by responding to the question "Will ye also go away?" (John 6:67). With Peter, we also feel utterly dependent upon the Savior and Lord of our lives and can reply together with him, "Lord, to whom shall we go?" (v. 68). It is unthinkable that we would locate our hope, our treasure, our everything anywhere but in the Lord Jesus Christ. We may let Him down, but He will never let us down. And why us? Well, it was His good pleasure, His perfect will, His sovereign, divinely limited atonement.

Another truth worthy of much meditation is that Christ Jesus was the initiator of Andrew and Peter's Christian life: "he saw Simon and Andrew" (Mark 1:16). Peter and Andrew were responding to a command rather than of their own free will mulling over a series of options before deciding on Christ; "And straightway they forsook their nets, and followed him" (v.18). When we put this together with the later chapters in John in which something of God's eternal Triune counsel is conveyed to us, His elect ones, this is of deep significance and ought to humble us to the dust, rendering us ever more the servant of our Master who said:

"And now, O Father, glorify thou me with thine own self with the glory which I had with thee before the world was. I have manifested thy name unto the men which thou gavest me out of the world: thine they were, and thou gavest them me; and they have kept thy word" (John 17:5-6). If it were not for His glorious, miraculous, specific, limited atonement, not a soul upon this earth would ever be saved.

Verses referred to

Mark 1:16, 18,

Luke 5:8

John 1:41, 6:67—68, 17:5—6

God in the flesh

Andrew you were extra earnest,
holy words did in your ear nest,
then you rushed back to your brother,
looking not to self but other.

Simon you weren't overcome,
you walked to Him, you'd later run,
and then the curious change of name,
He looked at you, you felt the same.

Andrew you were so obedient,
practical yet not expedient,
knowing you had found Messiah,
fishing brother from the fire.

Simon, restless when at dock,
you lived in boats you loved to rock,
you were ordained to realize,
God in the flesh, before your eyes!

Irresistible grace 1

If the Gospel message of salvation could be condensed into three words, then Come to Christ would be an adequate synopsis. There is no cold fatalism to be found in God's plan for wretched, moribund sinners. In every aspect; the glory of creation, the pangs of conscience, the curious events of providence, the authority of verbal inspiration, and the global witness of Spirit-filled believers, there is a powerful incentive to Come to Christ, no matter who you are or what you've done.

Even in the last few verses of the entire Bible; after the terrifying and solemn visions of a great red dragon, a great white throne and the lake of fire, there are the heartfelt and holy commands to Come and "take the water of life freely" (Rev 22:17). More encouraging still is the fact that such a command is aimed not at a moral elite but at "whosoever will" (v.17). In fact, "he that believeth on him is not condemned . . ." (John 3:18) even *now*, regardless of what you've done or how you've lived. Yes—you.

And yet, can the God who declares that "the world through him might be saved" (John 3:17) be the same God who, bar Noah's family, brought "the flood upon the world of the ungodly" (2 Pet 2:5)? Well, He can be if we see all the events of world history as part of a war set in motion in those early chapters of Creation; between "her seed" fulfilled in the Lord Jesus Christ, and "thy seed" of that deadly fallen angel, Lucifer (Gen 3:15).

This war will not go on forever; along with Noah, those who have "found grace in the eyes of the LORD" (Gen 6:8) are safe in the promised "seed". Those who "are of *your* father the devil" (John 8:44) are of the cursed "seed". Meanwhile, the "whosoever will" is for all seeds who are still breathing upon the face of this earth. If you are "athirst" (Rev 22:17) and your ears are wanting to hear more, this could be you. Why not you?

Verses referred to

Genesis 3:15, 6:8

2 Peter 2:5

John 3:17—18, 8:44

Revelation 22:17

Come to Christ

Come to Christ, not Go to Hell
God's call to those in spirit poor,
for man is but a dying well
whose bucket lies upon the floor.

Not Go to Hell, but Come to Christ
is what the Gospel message is,
for grace is free but sin is priced
man's credit zero, glory His.

Come to Christ, Go not to Hell
we need to hear now, before death,
for if we hear it all is well
and when we feel it, gone is death.

Go not to Hell, but Come to Christ
and yet so many will not come,
Christ kept back naught, Self sacrificed
what's keeping you? . . . oh sinner, Come.

Perseverance of the saints 1

When David declares, under inspiration of the Holy Spirit, how much he loves or delights in God's moral law multiple times in the same extended psalm (119), we must also ask ourselves if we love God's moral law, "for he *is* a Jew, which is one inwardly; and circumcision *is that* of the heart, in the spirit, *and* not in the letter . . ." (Rom 2:29). Indeed, it cannot be animal sacrifices or dietary-judicial laws that David is talking about, so much as the moral law which reveals something of the character of our Heavenly Father.

I confess that my grasp and love of the character of God (in the first table) is more superficial than I had hitherto thought. As for the second table—my duty to man—I feel I have not fulfilled "the law of Christ. For if a man think himself to be something, when he is nothing, he deceiveth himself" (Gal 6:2-3). However, like David I still love to read about God's transcendent holiness and, in Christ, mourn my failings, believing my Savior has entitled me no more to fear the law but rather to look upon it as a wondrous window into the attributes of God, a mirror revealing various aspects of my unworthy soul.

I know that only the Son of Man has truly lived out the law, practising what He preached in the Sermon on the Mount (Matt 5-7). However, I am also encouraged to *persevere* along the path of increasing mortification of sin and Christ-likeness, by those numerous saints of old and of present. Alas, I know how quickly the old nature in me would set the bar at a comfortable, easily achievable level, turning a blind eye to the "beam" of sin within (Matt 7:4).

Rather than be numbered with those who will be "weeping and wailing" (Rev 18:19) for worldly loss, may we be among those who "establish the law" (Rom 3:31) by looking unto the One who came "to fulfil" it (Matt 5:17), setting the bar of obedience upon the frame of love, for the Jesus we say we love has elevated His moral law to new heights, urging us keep it through Him, for His sake: "If ye love me, keep my commandments" (John 14:15).

Verses referred to

Psalm 119

Matthew 5:17, 7:4

John 14:15

Romans 2:29, 3:31

Galatians 6:2—3

Revelation 18:19

Thy law

I love Thy law which judges me
for in Thy law myself I see,
I outwardly appear alright
but inwardly pollute Thy light.

I love Thy law which guideth me
for in Thy law I learn to be,
if not, I'd always ever burn
with Lot's wife, staring, no return.

I love Thy law which follows me
for in Thy law I mercy see
forgiveness so unmerited,
through Christ alone, inherited.

I love Thy law which showeth me
for in Thy law I'm really me,
I'm whittled down on daily lathe,
I'm quickened through repenting faith.

Sola scriptura 2

It is remarkable that the Lord Jesus fasted for forty days; even more remarkable that during this time he was being ceaselessly "tempted of the devil" (Luke 4:2). As with His baptism, the lesson of the three recorded temptations is of great and ongoing practical importance for all believers.

First, the devil attacks our *priorities*. Knowing that "every word of God" (v.4) is indeed precious to the true believer, he subtly endeavors to get us to minor in the word of God and major in the "bread alone" (v.4), so that the things of this world increasingly become our main priority. It is his desire for us to become fruitless believers, in a bid to stop God's treasure from influencing our earthly lives and the lives of others.

Second, he attacks our fundamental *purpose* in life's journey. Under the guise of outwardly respectable, prestigious yet time-sapping worldly opportunities, the devil will promise us all "this power" (v.6) so long as we become progressively cooler toward the edifying things of God, eg. Bible study, prayer, fellowship, meditation, daily devotion. These things are not soul-saving but soul-nourishing. The devil knows that.

Third, he attacks our *perseverance*. The third temptation is the only one of the three in which he fully quotes Scripture. Yet he twists things in such a way that the duty of zealous, heartfelt perseverance in Christ gets transmogrified into a lukewarm wallowing in God's preservation of us, as we presume upon Him "to keep" us (v.10) while we aim to do nothing in particular for Him.

Our true and proper resting-place should be *sola Scriptura*, as seen in the way in which a (humanly speaking) drained Jesus faithfully recites three verses from the Torah (Deuteronomy). Our blessedness and usefulness in God's kingdom will abound as we consciously seek to live more and more "by every word of God" (v.4), resisting the temptation to hastily cherry-pick our favorite parts while carelessly ignoring the precious rest which we are told is all inspired; God-breathed.

Verses referred to

Luke 4:1–13

The Stronger

Satan, man's greatest opponent
Satan, sin's primal exponent,
was defeated at the Cross
as promised—bruised; eternal loss.

Satan, scripturally well versed
our ancient foe, tempting, rehearsed,
yet not a match for Christians true
a pied piper of rats untrue.

Satan, leading souls astray
most fears the soul which starts to pray,
the rest like pigs within his palace
blindly snort at Bible's arras.

Satan, mocker of the Christ
did tempt Him thrice but realized,
that through the cost of Calvary
the Stronger purchased victory.

Sola fide 2

There are some notably stalwart examples of faith throughout church history; the apostle Paul or Martin Luther come to mind, in which there is no doubt they were 100% all for the Lord, each a willing bondservant or slave of Christ, *bound* to do His will in that term's exalted sense. For most Christians, though, I would think that such clarity and Christ-centeredness is not quite so apparent in the hurly burly of everyday life. There are seasons of great zeal followed by seasons of relative coldness; times in which the heart seems to be on fire for the Lord; others when a choice has to be made or there is a conflict (providentially arranged) which forces one to take a stand or, if not, to fall and have to repent.

"Whom have I in heaven *but thee*? and *there is* none upon earth *that* I desire beside thee" (Ps 73:25) is the cry of a believer whose "feet were almost gone", whose "steps had well nigh slipped" (v. 2); the thoughts of a soul who realized the only important thing in life was to know the Lord and walk in His ways. If the heart has never fallen in love with God then there is only coldness and deadness, which will tragically manifest itself over time. Lot's wife, for example, "became a pillar of salt" (Gen 19:26) because, spiritually speaking, her heart was *already* a rocky wasteland devoid of the love of God. Her turning away from the Lord was not a shock but rather the culmination of the habit of a lifetime's inward rebellion.

Perhaps the hardest thing to repent of is one's own righteousness. Paul in Philippians 3 explains how *self* "confidence", "trust", being "circumcised", his ethnic "stock", his "Benjamin-Hebrew-Pharisee" pedigree, "zeal" and "righteousness" (v. 4-6) were terrible stumbling-blocks which had to be seen for what they were—worthless idols, before he found faith in Christ, thenceforth to live in a righteousness not his own.

How many in our day are proud of being of their race, nationality, gender, class or status? How many look in the mirror and instead of seeing a wretched sinner behold a decent, good enough person? If these things ring true for you, dear reader, may you start to throw them out of the basket of your life. May Christ fill you with the air of true faith, that you may ascend progressively heavenward through faith in Him.

Verses referred to

Genesis 19:26

Psalm 73:2, 25

Philippians 3:4—6

Slave

Slave of Satan, slave of Christ
no free will, third way, one or other,
son of Satan, son of Christ
living for self, or sister-brother.

Serving sin or serving Christ
no middle path, one of the two,
married to sin, married to Christ
the single life you cannot do.

Loving Mammon, loving Christ
no compromise, you can't love both,
dying for gain, alive in Christ
gaining just loss, eternal growth.

Born of Adam, born of Christ
no birth without inheritance,
this world wide web ensnared the Christ
His breaking—our deliverance.

Sola gratia 2

How dare any one of us become in any way proud or puffed up, in the light of the apostle Paul's philosophical question, "what hast thou that thou didst not receive?" (1 Cor 4:7) Can any of us have any cause for pride? Were we not rescued from our own ground zero, our own futile terrorist plot against God's holiness?

If the blessed and mightily used Isaiah felt moved to say of himself "Woe *is* me!" (Isa 6:5), how much more should *we* be being self-critical, self-analytical, ready to repent and turn to Christ; we who live in the amazing aftermath of His becoming incarnate and going to the Cross in lieu of us?

In fact, only the Person of persons can lawfully lay claim to having truly "loved righteousness, and hated iniquity" (Heb 1:9). Can any of us truthfully say the same? But surely our prayers, our faith, our grace-filled attitudes might be looked upon with some pleasure in heaven? Not according to the Scriptures, for Christ "ever liveth to make intercession" (Heb 7:25) for us who are in such continual and desperate need of it. Indeed, "the Spirit itself maketh intercession for us" (Rom 8:26), without whom we would have neither inclincation nor capacity for meaningful prayer.

I might despair, sometimes, seeing I cannot find within myself anything good, discovering the "sin that dwelleth in me" (Rom 7:17) which spoils my happiness and well-being. But then I remember that "I live; yet not I, but Christ liveth in me" (Gal 2:20)—He is my hope and salvation. I ought no longer trust in my own works to please the Lord, "otherwise grace is no more grace" (Rom 11:6). And I am no passive victim being ripped in half by opposing forces, for I prayerfully, actively, by God's gracious work within rather than my graceless brains and brawn strive not to "frustrate the grace of God" (Gal 2:21).

Verses referred to

Isaiah 6:5

Romans 7:17, 8:26, 11:6

1 Corinthians 4:7

Galatians 2:20—21

Hebrews 1:9, 7:25

Just the Son

My soul was rescued from the rubble
nothing in me, only trouble,
sin is gone but clouds remain
His type was Abel, mine was Cain.

My soul was salvaged from the pit
I couldn't stand, I wouldn't sit,
when He did shine His light in me
my filthy rags I first did see.

My soul was placed upon the Rock
a new-born soul, naked, in shock,
to drink from His redeeming well
was all I could do, all was well.

My soul is in His holy hand
although I rarely understand,
that not one thing I've ever done
has pleased the Father, just the Son.

Solo Christo 2

The glory of Christ is at times overwhelming; our words cannot do Him justice. Take Colossians 1, for example, where in our English translation the grammatical particles ascend increasingly to express the pre-existing, perpetual operation and activity of Christ in both the original creation and still more glorious regeneration: "of" (v. 13), "in" (v. 14), "through" (v. 14) "by" (v. 16), "for" (v. 16), "before" (v. 17), "in" (v. 19).

This is followed by the wondrous fact of us being "In the body of his flesh" (v. 22), "in his sight" (v. 22), of "Christ in my flesh" (v. 24), "Christ in you" (v. 27), "perfect in Christ Jesus" (v. 28). It is as if there is no higher form of grammatical closeness and intimacy which can be employed to express the amazing, exalted, surprising condition of finding oneself a Christian.

It reminds me of the apostle's inability to express his paradisiacal experience which he describes as being "unspeakable" and "not lawful for a man to utter" (2 Cor 12:4). But praise God that this is so, for the body of Christ, unlike the organizations and cultures of the world, brings the wretched, unworthy sinner into mutually loving, fulsome fellowship with the seasoned, sanctified saint.

Surely all we who were once individually and corporately blinded by the "god of this world" (2 Cor 4:4) may now say together, by God's grace, that whatever losses, crosses or failings we may endure in this world, "we have the mind of Christ" (1 Cor 2:16). It would be such a stupendously arrogant and presumptuous claim to make, if it were not true.

Verses referred to

1 Corinthians 2:16

2 Corinthians 4:4, 12:4

Colossians 1:13—14, 16—17, 19, 22, 24, 27—28

Christ's

Oh everything's now second best
for I have entered holy rest,
my old attachments have come loose
He's taken off my worldly noose.

Oh everything's been made anew
as Jesus Christ ever foreknew,
that I'd one day see I was lost
I'd realize what sin has cost.

Oh everything's been reconciled
the Son in my place was reviled,
was offered up for all my sins
old things have died, new life begins.

Oh everything's now last not first
for holy water now I thirst,
I'm hungry for the bread of life
I earn no living, Christ's my life.

Soli Deo Gloria 2

There is the eternal glory of the Godhead which existed before creation came into being: "And now, O Father, glorify thou me with thine own self with the glory which I had with thee before the world was" (John 17:5). There is the glory of the unfallen, created, angelic order, which neither knew separation nor banishment from its Creator: "And one cried unto another, and said, Holy, holy, holy, *is* the Lord of hosts: the whole earth is full of his glory" (Isa 6:3). There is the glory of the fallen image bearers, willingly intoned from the heart of every redeemed sinner who has been made a saint through the meritorious work of Another: "But the God of all grace, who hath called us unto his eternal glory by Christ Jesus, after that ye have suffered a while, make you perfect, stablish, strengthen, settle *you*" (1 Pet 5:10).

Then there is the glory of recognizing Christ, in which every fallen image bearer must "confess that Jesus Christ *is* Lord, to the glory of God the Father" (Phil 2:11). And there is the glory which men strive to withhold and deny, but which nevertheless is: "And men were scorched with great heat, and blasphemed the name of God, which hath power over these plagues: and they repented not to give him glory" (Rev 16:9). This glory is a glory which demonstrates the sovereignty of the Creator, the awful power and majesty of the Being through whom all things have had and have their being.

Yet the notion of *glory* is not one which resonates in that awful place of separation; hell. For the reflected glory of God in sinners saved shall be brought into the new heaven and new earth: "And they shall bring the glory and honour of the nations into it" (Rev 21:26), although reference to God's glory, though necessarily present in the righteous judgement of impenitent sinners, is *negatively* rather than *positively* affirmed, present through its absence from the fulness of God's joyful glory in that infinitely better place: "there shall in no wise enter into it any thing that defileth, neither *whatsoever* worketh abomination, or *maketh* a lie: but they which are written in the Lamb's book of life" (Rev 21:27).

May the Lord graciously draw in many more souls through the blessed and only Door before the end shall come. Although He will ultimately have all the glory, both in mercy *and* in judgement, yet He delights in answering our foreordained prayers, taking "no pleasure in the death of the wicked; but that the wicked turn from his way and live . . ." (Ezek 33:11).

Verses referred to

Isaiah 6:3

Ezekiel 33:11

John 17:5

Philippians 2:11

1 Peter 5:10

Revelation 16:9, 21:26–27

The point of no return

Every foul, ungodly pleasure
every time of stolen leisure,
will be paid for, after death
in hellish climes' infernal breath.

Every chance to turn and seek
all times the Lord did seem to speak,
will be charged to your soul's account
your living death, the full amount.

Every pang of conscience killed
impenitence, deceit self willed,
will be forever dwelled upon
God's image lost, yet never gone.

Every thought of gratitude
despised among the multitude,
will be in hell, no mercy, how?
rejecting Christ, you're Satan's now.

Total depravity 2

From Babel to Nasa, mankind has striven not merely to live, to exist, to prosper but to transcend, to do good; not content to be in the image of God but, preposterously, to rival God! Our claims of cold-blooded rational enlightenment are belied by our behavior, which everywhere cries worship! adore! idolize! follow! Sadly, it has taken a twisted turn and there are now core areas of human existence (eg. marriage, justice, education, science) in which those Creation ordinances of Genesis are barely recognizable; prophesied in advance by God's word in 2 Timothy 3:1-7.

The fall of part of the angelic order in this regard may be illuminating, in that the implied Lucifer, son of the morning, is described by the inspired prophet as being self-corrupted "because of" his "beauty" and "by reason of" his "brightness" (Ezek 28:17). It was as if the capacity of the creature could not handle the greatness of the attributes with which it was endowed, hence would serve as a lesson for us—to be content with the condition in which we find ourselves. Contentment is one of the great hallmarks of godliness and is a scarce and precious commodity.

Likewise, the fall of the human order can be instructive in that it came about not merely because of the beauty and prospect of ingesting something hidden or extra. Rather, our self-corruption came about due to our staggeringly hubristic desire to "be as gods" (Gen 3:5), and "to make *one* wise" (v.6), as if being created, blessed and privileged in Eden were not enough!

Just about every movie and video game created these days hints at a general discontentment with the human condition, a desire to transcend it via super-human, techno-miraculous transformation. This fallen world is in desperate need of heeding the only and true King's commands, which alone can help put us in our rightful place, revealing our common mortality: "Put them in fear, O LORD: *that* the nations may know themselves *to be but* men" (Ps 9:20). The saved children of God are also shepherded away from any hint of worldly-minded self-reliance: "Know ye that the Lord he *is* God: *it is* he *that* hath made us, and not we ourselves; *we are* his people, and the sheep of his pasture" (Ps 100:3). It is to our shame that we need to be told this.

Verses referred to

Genesis 3:5—6

Psalm 9:20, 100:3

Ezekiel 28:17

2 Timothy 3:1—7

This dying world

To threaten man's autonomy
his third world false economy,
is that which truly does offend
for then his rule of self must end.

To say this is a dying world
the remedy in Christ unfurled,
upsets the human applecart
our kingdoms perishing with art.

To say we're sinners from the Fall
that Adam sinned so then did all,
upends our seesaw of good deeds
sending us to Another's deeds.

To threaten man with punishment
is what the world thought Moses meant,
but Jesus came to die for you
in Him you die to rise anew.

Unconditional election 2

I cannot help but think of Ezekiel's vision of dry bones, the bones representing us in our fallen, spiritual condition . . . 100% lifeless. As God questions Ezekiel, "Son of man, can these bones live?" (37:3) He goes on to describe His breathing of life into the skeletal, thus reminding us of His original first creation. At no point is there any agency in the bones, any merit in them, any decision required by them. The Lord's conclusion is that "then shall ye know that I the LORD have spoken *it*, and performed *it*" (v. 14), this lesson being as vital to receive as it is impossible to learn without divine operation.

We may recall old Simeon's prophecy near the beginning of the New Testament, revealing how Christ's ministry would first have to destroy before creating, first level before raising up, He being "set for the fall and rising again of many in Israel" (Luke 2:34). A preacher once put it this way; his struggle was not so much to get people saved as to get them lost, that they might then see their need of being truly saved!

How Christ divides opinion, whether in religious or political circles, His identity and Gospel being "a sign which shall be spoken against" (v. 34)! If there is one thing on which the present-day Eastern Islamist and Western hedonist can agree, it is that the Bible is not true and that Christ, if he existed, cannot save and cannot be personally known. So it was with Gentile Pilate and Jewish Herod, who were made friends (Luke 23:12) by their mutual denial of Christ.

True believers, however, accept and even rejoice in their impotence and God's unconditional election of them. Unlike the Herods and Pilates of this world, they are made to realize that they can "have no power" in anything, physical or spiritual, except it be given "from above" (John 19:11). Thus, all they may seek to do *for* Him must come *from* Him. He gets the glory; not us.

Verses referred to

Ezekiel 37:3, 14   John 19:11

Luke 2:34, 23:12

39

Praying saint

Vile, wicked, evil creature
minus one redeeming feature,
yet the Lord of glory came
to wrap my soul up in His name.

Selfish, sinful, lustful person
in the flesh which can but worsen,
yet the Lord of mercy wrought
a work in me so far from thought.

Hardened, willful, secret being
ever looking, never seeing,
till the point my sin I saw
enriched in Christ, in spirit poor.

Grateful, groaning, praying saint
a truth I could not dream or paint,
a sinner saved, now to be used
by God, in Christ forever fused.

Limited atonement 2

That beautiful and profound verse, "And they glorified God in me" (Gal 1:24) says so much in so few words. It was not Paul they glorified, nor his racial or facial profile. In fact, Pharisee Saul had been a sworn enemy and persecutor of the early followers of Christ, which made it all the more remarkable that God should turn him around, entering into and transforming him through the Holy Spirit. Why him? What did he have to offer, other than oppression, enmity, and hatred? For that matter, what do we have to offer?

To the non-believer, there would have been no glorifying. To the Jewish religionist of the day, Pharisee Saul (now Paul) would have been an embarrassment, a heretic worthy of being stoned to death. To the local Roman or Greek citizen, he would simply have been an obnoxious *other* from an ethnic minority. Yet to every born-again believer there is that measure of glorifying God; in Paul, in themselves, in all elect souls who have been and are being transformed by Christ. With each and every one, human speaking, it seemed so unlikely that such a thing would ever be.

Early on in one's walk with God there may be more stumbling and meandering. Sadly, this can also happen later on. When the house of Ephraim and Judah, for example, saw his "sickness" and "wound", ie. when the tried believer is troubled by some inward sin or outward trial, "then went Ephraim to the Assyrian, and sent to king Jareb: yet he could not heal you, nor cure you of your wound" (Hos 5:13). The world has nothing with which to bind up your wounds, to cure your broken heart. It is a painful lesson we learn all too slowly. We must be gradually weaned off dependence on this world's ways, learning to lean more trustingly upon our Heavenly Father.

Whether it be money or health, job or family, persecution or backsliding, let us remember the Son's atonement for us; an *us* chosen and limited from His sovereign view, yet countless as the stars from our earthly view. When we turn to the only solution, the only balm for the soul's aches and pains, then like "Ephraim" you "*shall say,* What have I to do any more with idols? I have heard *him,* and observed him: I *am* like a green fir tree. From me is thy fruit found" (Hos 14:8).

Let us pray that others may glorify God in us, and that we may increasingly lay aside that competitive, envious spirit which is of the world. We now have nothing more to prove; our God has atoned for us, plucked us as brands out of the fire, led us in another way from the way to which we were hellbent on going.

Verses referred to

Hosea 5:13, 14:8

Galatians 1:24

Your worldly friends

Your worldly friends once close, now far
as God in you they hate, revile,
once your old sword with theirs did spar
but now they slay you with a smile.

Your worldly friends round in on you
thinking you're fake, that they're all right,
but really they abhor your view
they follow darkness, you Christ's light.

Your worldly friends all play a game
believing sin's not what one is,
they're not guilty, will have no blame
if God exists then God love is.

Your worldly friends can't see your point
behind your back they stab your life,
Christ only can a soul anoint
—believe God's blood, beware Lot's wife.

Irresistible grace 2

The Holy Spirit silently does His work when all seems lost. Picture in your mind the prodigal son, alone and bereft of all human companionship, poignantly described thus: "he came to himself" (Luke 15:17). What soul on earth has ever come to itself (its sense of having wronged a holy, heavenly Father) without God the Spirit first working in that heart?

We may think of the stubborn unbelief and blindness of the human heart outside of Christ. We concur with David when he says, "in thy light shall we see light" (Ps 36:9), for there was a time when we did not see spiritual things, when the Bible's many pages seemed a distant, inscrutable hinterland. Then, a time "when it pleased God, who separated me from my mother's womb, and called *me* by his grace, to reveal his Son in me" (Gal 1:15-16). What made the difference, or rather, Who? The Triune God, of course.

We treasure the glorious words of the Scriptures, especially the crowning glory of the Old Testament revealed, ie. the New Testament. But what of them? Were they devised through the minds and traditions of subjective, prejudiced men? No, for as Christ Himself explains, the Comforter was to come and Himself write the New Testament through the pens of chosen men (John 14:26) who often depicted themselves in a less than flattering light. Is the *Old* Testament nothing but the culturally benighted prelude to the more precise and loving *New*? Not at all, "for the prophecy came not in old time by the will of man: but holy men of God spake *as they were* moved by the Holy Ghost" (2 Pet 1:21).

What glorious thoughts, then, to read that we were irresistibly drawn by the Father to the Son through the Spirit (Acts 1:7–8); what unspeakable joy to know that we are not left alone after conversion but are in-dwelt by God the Spirit throughout our entire Christian lives: "the Spirit also helpeth our infirmities: for we know not what we should pray for as we ought: but the Spirit itself maketh intercession for us with groanings which cannot be uttered" (Rom 8:26).

If we *were* left alone, who among us would not inevitably return to "the husks that the swine did eat" (Luke 15:16)?

Verses referred to

Psalm 36:9

Luke 15:16–17

John 14:26

Acts 1:7–8

Romans 8:26

Galatians 1:15—16

2 Peter 1:21

The Spirit's

The Spirit's undeniable,
though here, unquantifiable,
for when you're truly born again,
your former self becomes a den
of wolves now tame which once were wild,
you're Spirit led, at bottom mild
and nothing to Him can compare,
He's God, your
interceding prayer.

The Spirit's irresistible,
though here, all but insensible,
for your self interest now has cooled,
it's Christ you look to, no more fooled,
on dry land His in fellowship,
you're Spirit led, off world-wor-ship,
and nothing to Him can you add,
He's willing you to
make God glad.

The Spirit's of the Trinity,
though here, He is Divinity,
for when you cry out to the Lord,
your spirit chimes with Spirit's chord,
your heart awaits His special note,
you're Spirit led, you didn't vote,
and nothing from Him can you draw,
but Jesus Christ,
forevermore.

Perseverance of the saints 2

"And Asahel pursued after Abner; and in going he turned not to the right hand nor to the left from following Abner" (2 Sam 2:19).

It is possible to pursue earnestly, zealously and yet not according to wisdom. There are many things one might like to pursue that may not be of the Lord. One's *Abner* might seemingly be for the greater glory of God's kingdom but might not be God's will for you. How many evangelical churches contain young men who dream of being a pastor; yet how many of those young men are not called to be a pastor and so fritter away their valuable time hankering after something to which they were never called?

One's *Abner* might be something of a more secular nature; career advancement, personal success, health, wealth, or happiness. It is not the Lord's will for these things to be pursued at the expense of increasingly honest and heartfelt daily devotions, simple trust in Christ Jesus, loyal and regular fellowship with local brethren. That is not to say that such things do not have their place, but to obsessively pursue them at all costs is foolish.

As the Lord beckons us through another year may we each more honestly review our lives, prayerfully identifying false pursuits, dead ends, fleshly and satanic distractions, so that we may not pursue our particular *Abners* but "Jesus the author and finisher of *our* faith; who for the joy that was set before him endured the cross, despising the shame, and is set down at the right hand of the throne of God" (Heb 12:2). He alone is worth pursuing. When push comes to shove we must have Him, above all else.

Verses referred to

2 Samuel 2:19

Hebrews 12:2

Fine yourself

Speed camera Christian, please slow down
don't speed away from Christ today,
your destination's up not down
your hellish fine His death did pay.

Oh office Christian, gossip not
don't listen as they tear apart,
pray for their souls, don't join their rot
repent they must or will depart.

Oh Sunday Christian, please sit down
don't worship worship, turn today
to Him Who came from heaven down
to turn us from our hellbound way.

Nominal Christian, offer not
your righteousness, your filthy rags,
depend upon the Savior's lot
He's making mansions, leave your bags.

Sola scriptura 3

The Bible is a living book and so the human spirit cannot endure it unless the Holy Spirit works within—the Word and the Spirit speak as one. Unlike a worldly film or novel which usually leads us to identify with a hero, despise a villain, the Bible reads *us*, troubles us, cuts us to the core: "For the word of God *is* quick, and powerful, and sharper than any twoedged sword, piercing even to the dividing asunder of soul and spirit, and of the joints and marrow, and *is* a discerner of the thoughts and intents of the heart" (Heb 4:12).

The Bible is an intimate book like no other, which draws us to the person of the Lord Jesus Christ, about whom the whole Book is, upon whom the whole Book rests. It is possible to study the Bible, know its historical, cultural, linguistic heritage and yet be a stranger in it. Like reading the love letter of a soldier in World War 1 it may appear a musty, agèd thing not intended for modern consumption. However, it is actually an intensely personal message from the only true Knower and Lover of your soul: "Search the scriptures; for in them ye think ye have eternal life: and they are they which testify of me. And ye will not come to me, that ye might have life" (John 5:39-40). The problem is not with the Sender but with the human heart, because the intensely personal message challenges it to respond in repentance which in its pride it cannot. Thus, we hold this Book at arm's length, fending off its troubling, penetrating gaze.

Like receiving an important e-mail which you know will have deep consequences and implications, even a believer may at times be reticent about opening up God's Word. However, there is always more encouragement, wisdom and uplift to be found within its pages than we tend to recall; it will always ring truer than any other source of comfort or information this side of eternity. It also has a special cleansing power since in no other way can both our fundamental sin *and* our daily sins be purged: "Now ye are clean through the word which I have spoken unto you" (John 15:3). It is something we need to keep returning to so as to keep receiving fresh cleansings. Indeed, this 'I' (of John 15:3) is nothing less than the belovèd 'Word' who delights in communing with us as we draw ever nearer to Him.

Verses referred to

John 5:39—40, 15:3   Hebrews 4:12

Oh watch

Oh watch them place Him in a manger
out of harm's way, free from danger,
though the Christ who lives and reigns
foresaw it all from heaven's plains.

Oh watch them place Him on a cross
embalm in varnish, wood emboss,
Christ knoweth every sin in time
leaving them in their pantomime.

Oh watch them place Him in a book
demeaning Him by hook or crook,
God omnipotent keeps His promise
sheep as wolves betray His premise.

Oh watch them crucify His name
religion to them's just a game,
turn back from pomp and circumstance
oh search for Him, sit out this dance.

Sola fide 3

We are exhorted to take "the shield of faith" in Ephesians 6:16, for it is only as we see ourselves in Scripture that we see ourselves at all. Only when the world's twisted, ungodly images of us are filtered out and deflected do we begin to see ourselves as God sees us, living gradually more Christly lives. The first four of God's ten commandments can help us to do this, if we look at them through faith's lens:

1. "Thou shalt have no other gods before me" (v.3) can help us deal with the blinding light of Satan, outlined in 2 Corinthians 4:4. As one thinks upon the 1st commandment and how Christ alone has fully kept it, the Christian mind is protected by faith from beholding other gods which may ruin one's testimony, making "shipwreck" of one's "faith" (1 Tim 1:19).

2. "Any likeness *of any thing*" (v.4) refers to that intimate connection between eye and mind, linking the 1st with the 2nd commandment. Anything which could distract us from beholding more and more of God's glory is to be put away, held at arm's length, never embraced or coveted. We are "in the world" (John 17:11) but "not of the world" (v.14), a paradox understood by faith.

3. The tongue, that instrument by which souls are saved (Rom 10:14) can be a source of evil if abused (Jas 3:8). "In vain" (Exod 20:7) surely applies to unbelievers and believers alike, in that a loose and a shallow use of God's name are both abominated. The "unsearchable riches of Christ" (Eph 3:8) can never be exhausted, and so must mean the uttering of His name be done thoughtfully and reverently.

4. Behind the mind, eye, and tongue dwells the person. Our whole walk is to be interrupted and checked, one day in seven. We are to "Remember" (v.8) God more exclusively in order that our weekly approach to life become more regulated by His will, not our own. As our bodies rest more fully from worldly things, so our souls become more fully alive.

Thus, the shield of faith is the whole word of God; turned to, opened up, meditated on by the persevering, forgiven Christian soldier: "He layeth up sound wisdom for the righteous: *he is* a buckler to them that walk uprightly" (Prov 2:7).

Verses referred to

Exodus 20:3—11

Proverbs 2:7

John 17:11, 14

Romans 10:14

2 Corinthians 4:4

Ephesians 3:8, 6:16

1 Timothy 1:19

James 3:8

The mask

The mask that slowly we become
is shattered at conversion,
the sinful clay we used to love
is now to us coercion.

Meanwhile the world is still at work
forming its Babel version,
our roles are scripted day to day
to God there is aversion.

The uniforms we tend to wear
are styled in Satan's vision,
from coats to hats to skirts to jeans
we mirror television.

And yet God is longsuffering
so patient in His mission,
your narrative needs saving faith
without it, there's perdition.

Sola gratia 3

When one goes through that experience of being born again, it is almost a thing of sadness to contemplate returning to the world from which one was plucked, there being an urge "to depart, and to be with Christ; which is far better" (Phil 1:23). However, it is God's good pleasure that we do return to live to His glory; He gives believers in Christ the latter half of His moral law to help with their heavenward pilgrimage, by grace through faith, devoid of human merit:

5. The "honour" (Exod 20:12) due to parents is a solemn one, because *that* relationship more than any other represents the relationship of our Father to a chosen soul. The closeness of mother to baby or father to child cannot be equaled by other versions of relationship (teacher-student, employer-employee) which can but reflect it.

6. We can "kill" (v.13) in many ways; verbally, socially, emotionally, politically, militarily. There is, of course, such a thing as a just cause. However, in terms of daily living we kill when we are angry "without a cause" (Matt 5:22), so one is to consider the inverse of this commandment, graciously seeking to "love your enemies" (v.44) without cause! Such causeless love reflects the causeless love that Christ had and has for you, who didn't and don't deserve it.

7. "Adultery" (v.14), whilst impossible for the true believer to desire or dwell in, is nevertheless a temptation which serves as a barometer of our spiritual temperature. When prayers and Bible reading dry up, adultery will come a-knocking, the spiritual being the precursor to the mental; then, God forbid, the bodily.

8. To "steal" (v.15) by the use of tongue, hand, mind, means to unlawfully build up a private Babel away from God, and can happen in the realm of work, play, even religion. When Christ the Lord is not the ultimate object of our desire, we steal away our gifts from Him, needing again to give ourselves back to our High Priest as "a living sacrifice" (Rom 12:1).

9. To "bear false witness" (v.16) is, for the believer, to live a life which is indistinguishable from that of a worldly unbeliever. If we allow ourselves to become the world's friend in the wrong sense (as opposed to the right sense), we are forfeiting the effectiveness of our witness and our privileged position as light bearers.

10. To "covet" (17) in itself is not a bad thing, for we are urged to "covet earnestly the best gifts" (1 Cor 12:31). However, if the eye does not fill itself with the best gifts (Bible, prayer, evangelistic outreach, Christian literature, God-honoring music, warm fellowship), it will inevitably covet the worst gifts which may end up becoming punishments amid their vain pleasures.

May the Lord bless us along our solitary journeys, as by His grace we become less like ourselves and more like Him.

Verses referred to

Exodus 20:12—17	1 Corinthians 12:31
Matthew 5:22, 44	Philippians 1:23
Romans 12:1	

Thank God

Thank God God only knows the heart,
that bodies touch yet are apart,
for even in a new born's breast
the cold war rumbles, far from rest.

Thank God God only knows the mind,
that even to ourselves we're blind,
for even in a new born's head
there is a struggle, sin though dead.

Thank God God only knows the soul,
that in our trials there is a goal,
for even in a new born's day
there dwells a darkness, held at bay.

Thank God God only knows the world,
before and after, all unfurled,
for all whose life is God the Son
there's forgiveness, under the sun.

Solo Christo 3

So many threats there are in this life as we "walk through the valley of the shadow of death" (Ps 23:4). Yet Christ Jesus overwhelms them all, being antitype, antithesis and antidote to all that the flesh, the world, and the devil can muster.

In Romans 8:35

When we face

"tribulation"	He is our "peace" (Eph 2:14),
"persecution"	He is our "advocate" (1 John 2:1),
"famine"	He is our "bread" (John 6:48),
"nakedness"	He is our "covert" (Isa 32:2),
"peril"	He is our "salvation" (Luke 2:30),
"sword"	He is our "Lion" (Rev 5:5).

In Romans 8:38

When we face

"death"	He is our "life" (Col 3:4),
"life"	He is the "stone" (Isa 8:14, 1 Pet 2:8),
"angels"	He is the "Father" (Isa 9:6),
"principalities"	He is our "head" (Col 2:10),
"powers"	He is our "power" (1 Cor 1:24),
"things present"	He is "eternal" (1 John 5:20),
"things to come"	He is the "I AM" (John 8:58).

In Romans 8:39

When we face

"height"	He is the "dayspring" (Luke 1:78),
"depth"	He is "God" (Isa 54:5),
"any other creature"	He is the only "begotten" (John 1:14, 1 John 4:9).

What more on earth or in heaven can we need!

Verses referred to

Psalm 23:4

Isaiah 8:14, 9:6, 32:2, 54:5

Luke 1:78, 2:30

John 1:14, 6:48, 8:58

Romans 8:35, 38—39

1 Corinthians 1:24

Ephesians 2:14

Colossians 2:10, 3:4

1 Peter 2:8

1 John 2:1, 4:9, 5:20

Revelation 5:5

Where Christ is

Oh blessèd exchange, so unfair,
the Sinless for the sinful stood,
each one of us in spirit there
we all are guilty, One is good.

Our Father's love is everlasting
not for mere religious folk,
all days of ritual, feast and fasting
can't clear sin, God must revoke.

Receivers of the second birth
rejoice beyond all mortal mud,
for you in Christ who've conquered earth
are heaven's now, by holy blood.

This wooden world says 'God is not,
that it just was, and so it is',
Pinocchios professing rot,
—our life is just—where Jesus is.

Soli Deo Gloria 3

It is a sad thing when a saint loses something of the passion, joy, and amazement of his or her "first love" (Rev 2:4). Daily duties, distractions, and preoccupations can enter in; it is therefore vital for us to regularly set before us something of God's glory. He alone has been responsible for transforming us from inwardly ugly subjects to heavenly-minded citizens. It wasn't anything to do with us.

The religious Pharisee Saul "fell to the earth" (Acts 9:4), "trembling and astonished" (v. 6), the sheer otherness of his encounter with the Lord Jesus overwhelming him. The intellectual prophet Isaiah felt "undone" and "unclean" (Isa 6:5) upon witnessing something of the transcendent glory of God. We may not have had identical experiences, but ought we not feel a similar sense of amazement and humility? Christ being the amazing reality of our existence, can't we attune ourselves to Him more accurately and often than we do?

Let us be mindful of the human infirmity of the belovèd John when he endeavored to bow before "the feet of the angel" (Rev 22:8), not long after worshiping Christ Jesus in the self-abasing reverence of someone "as dead" (Rev 1:17). Thankfully, the Master had already reassured him, commanding him to "Fear not" (v.17), encouraging us, too.

May we approach our Lord Jesus with appropriate godly fear and reverence, yet not in a craven way of impossible severity or strictness. May we, in all our Godward intentions, feelingfully remember the evangelistic "whosoever will, let him take the water of life freely" (Rev 22:17); "Alpha" words which may still be offered to "dogs, and sorcerers, and whoremongers, and murderers, and idolaters" (Rev 22:15) all the way until that blazing, glorious day of "Omega" (Rev 22:13).

Verses referred to

Isaiah 6:5   Revelation 1:17, 2:4, 6, 22:8, 13, 15, 17
Acts 9:4, 6

The overwhelming

Oh but the unapproachable light,
the utter trembling reality of it all,
when at His feet you fell
and felt what the sun
can but reflect!

Oh but the unspeakable holiness,
the tragic fallenness of us all,
when of His throne you heard
and could not stop hearing
Holy, holy, holy . . .

Oh but the awesome majesty,
the angel's face you did appall
when stumbling in worship
you faltered,
as do all.

Oh but the Alpha—Omega,
the justice, the judgement for
every one by One . . .
how every knee
shall bow!

Total depravity 3

The notion that a Christian has made not one millimeter of progress in the flesh, even years after conversion, is one which might be troubling. *Surely I'm a better person now than I was all those years ago?* one might reasonably ask. *Surely sin has less power over me, less attraction, less danger for me than it did before I was converted?*, are thoughts which might reasonably be posited by the reflective, Christian mind.

However, the answer is that in one sense there has been zero progress; you are as unable and vulnerable now as you were before, for "the body *is* dead because of sin" (Rom 8:10). Dead is dead and never can be made alive, never improved, never elevated in God's sight. "And if Christ *be* in you" (v.10) then this is so, for we are effectively put to death at conversion and stay dead all the way to glory.

When we pick up a Bible with sorrow or shame or expectation or hope, it is the Spirit leading us to do so. When we have a desire to enjoy Christian fellowship, go to church, hear a sermon, do an act of peculiar kindness, put a sinful thought or word to death, reach out to a soul with the Gospel, prayerfully collapse into our Father's arms, alter a plan because it seems not to be His will, dwell at length upon a particular portion of Scripture that seems to speak to us, it is because the "Spirit *is* life" (v.10) within us. The Spirit makes us alive because Christ is our life; in ourselves we remain spiritually dead—in Him alive.

Even as we are being led heavenward by the Spirit, our hearts, flesh, personalities, old natures, self-originating words, thoughts, and deeds remain "dead because of sin". A paradox in the world's mind is to the Christian the path of spiritual progress, the belief that I "can do all things through Christ which strengtheneth me" (Phil 4:13)—all things worth doing, that is, all things which are pleasing to God.

Verses referred to

Romans 8:10

Philippians 4:13

O wretched man

O wretched man, your root of sin
is not your deeds, your lose and win,
it's you at core who are at fault
you are a sinner by default.

O wretched man, your glory, power
wilts away, a fading flower,
look to God, the gardener
the source of souls, the pardoner.

O wretched man, sky scraping still
remember God did Babel still,
look now to Christ, you may be found
He meets with those of zero ground.

O wretched man, ignore man's poll,
Immanuel's your only goal,
for heaven knows we have no right,
we leave our darkness by His light.

Unconditional election 3

If "whatsoever things were written aforetime were written for our learn-
ing" . . . (Rom 15:4) and "beginning at Moses and all the prophets, he ex-
pounded unto them in all the scriptures the things concerning himself"
(Luke 24:27), we are surely to read the royal love story between Esther
and King Ahasuerus not merely as an isolated excerpt in the history of
the Jewish people, but as a profound illustration of Christ and His bride,
the 'elect' Church.

Esther, unlike the Queen of Sheba (illustrative of the seeking experience) is
described not as seeking but sought: "brought also unto the king's house"
(Esth 2:8), the Spirit-filled penman emphasizing how "he preferred her"
(2:9). A Christian, similarly, is not someone who has initiated a saving re-
lationship with God (although subjectively the seeking experience occurs)
but is one who has acted *in response to* the Holy Spirit's work within, de-
pendent wholly on Him. Christ Jesus reminds us that "Ye have not chosen
me, but I have chosen you" (John 15:16), there being no personal ground
for one's salvation other than the Sovereign's will.

Esther is described as having purified herself "with oil of myrrh" and "sweet
odours" (Esth 2:12), so that King Ahasuerus "delighted" in her (2:14) and
she "obtained favour in the sight of all them that looked upon her" (2:15).
The prayers of believers likewise are described as ascending "up before
God" with the "smoke of the incense" (Rev 8:4), the Lord shunning the
Vashtian vainglory of this world in favor of the "meek and quiet spirit"
(1 Pet 3:4) of the true Church. The *so* of "So Esther was taken unto king
Ahasuerus into his house royal" (Esth 2:16) bespeaks effectual calling. Like
us, Esther had her trials, doubts, difficulties, but ultimately obtained "grace
and favour in his sight" (Esth 2:17). True Christians find assurance not in
themselves but in God; being pleasing in His sight means everything.

For each believer there has been a time of willful, oblivious darkness, when
we were "without Christ, being aliens from the commonwealth of Israel,
and strangers from the covenants of promise, having no hope, and without
God in the world" (Eph 2:12). Who or what made the difference? Did we

of our own ability or volition one day just start to listen to our consciences? Was it our fledgling faith or gradual repentance which started to stack up points so as to grant us entry into His presence? A thousand times no, for salvation is "not of blood, nor of the will of the flesh, nor of the will of man, but of God" (John 1:13).

If you are a believer, nothing less than God's unconditional election of you is the cause of your belief. Nothing in you wanted the things which are of the King of kings, for in you are things "which war against the soul" (1 Pet 2:11). In fact, all of us who no longer walk as we used to but rather "as strangers and pilgrims" (v.11), have been summoned from the realm of the dead to the realm of the living, being elected to be citizens of God's holy kingdom. Surely there are many more to be raised up and clothed with a righteousness not their own before the end shall come.

Verses referred to

Esther 2:8—9, 12, 14—17

Luke 24:27

John 1:13, 15:16

Romans 15:4

Ephesians 2:12

1 Peter 2:11, 3:4

Revelation 8:4

In foreign righteousness

In foreign righteousness I stand
my soul by faith does understand,
that all my sins were put on Him
my life, though darkened, will not dim.

In godly judgement do I speak
within myself where all is weak,
for conscience brings to me my worst
wretched yet blessed, for Christ was cursed.

In alien holiness I think
all prayerful thoughts to Him I link,
and all my foolish thoughts are mine
amazing that He paid my fine.

In heaven's love I daily walk
a love beyond all human talk,
for by His blood He sprinkled us
who hate our lives, who love Jesus.

Limited atonement 3

In each era there are similar challenges to the Word of God, manifested in a variety of ways. In those blessed days when the Lord walked among us in the flesh, there was the point-blank unbelief of many who witnessed visible miracles occurring before their very eyes but who did not come to Christ for salvation. Ultimately, the reason for this was that they were not elect. They were left to their own devices, devices which can only lead to hell.

The Bible is a joyful but also solemn book. Solemn is the following reply to the those who crave outward signs or, as the so-called new atheists of our day might say, evidence: "But I said unto you, That ye also have seen me, and believe not." (John 6:36). No amount of visible evidence will satisfy or fulfil a sinner, demonstrated by those privileged freed slaves of Moses' day, for whom "the word preached did not profit them, not being mixed with faith in them that heard *it*" (Heb 4:2).

In these days of techno-dolatry, Western influenced culture seems to have intensified this need to have in our hands a body of unspecified 'evidence'. We are often led by the nose to consider the scientific evidence vs. religious faith debate, as if these are twin towers which cannot be truly reconciled. Here, though, the Lord addresses those who would make a god out of evidence, who would make 'evidence' the litmus test of faith as if the one can inevitably morph into the other, given enough time and weight. Some may be drawn out of rebellion, according to God's sovereign will. Many will left to their hearts' content, in this case the manmade devices of evolution and humanism, so-called.

The truth is, no matter how much evidence we have the human heart is hardened, deadened, resistant, desperately hostile to the gracious Light of the world. The evidence vs. faith debate is a strawman, a smokescreen which satanically blinds people to the true battle that has ancient origins. We *will* not come to Christ in submissive repentance and faith; we *will* not let the glorious light of conviction and conversion in; we *will* not admit or listen to the evidence of outward creation and inward conscience, because our hearts are full of rebellion, sin, and self-righteousness, loving "darkness rather than light" (John 3:19).

It is not that the Creator's salvation is thwarted by the creature, but that salvation is a sovereign thing which is entirely of God's (to us) mysterious will. There is no one who is excluded from the call to come to Christ, but as God has foreordained, many have excluded themselves by refusing to dwell upon the claims of the Bible, rendering it off limits, top secret, ruinous to their declaration of human independence. There will be an eternity for them to consider the unreasonableness and pig-headedness of their devices. They will see their folly for what it was, but will be given to dwell in bitterness, blame, belittling and begrudging of God. They will be fixed in their rebellion with no further possibility of redemption.

This needn't be you if you will but come to Him on His terms: "All that the Father giveth me shall come to me; and him that cometh to me I will in no wise cast out." (John 6:37). Repent, dear rebel. Repent and be saved, in the name of Jesus Christ.

Verses referred to

John 3:19, 6:36—7

Hebrews 4:2

Extremists

Blind Bartimaeus, short Zacchaeus,
simply were not satisfied,
one had too much, one not enough,
extremists both, we cast aside.

Then Christ the Lord came walking by,
one on Him spied, one to Him cried,
the Lord looked at each, rich and poor,
He took one's rags, the other's pride.

Blind Bartimaeus, faithfully,
got up as Christ drew him aside,
while short Zacchaeus, joyfully,
shared out his gold, with Christ inside.

How treacherous—the seeing eye,
inverting every image spied,
distorting all—the fallen mind,
a 'god' that says that God has lied!

Irresistible grace 3

It is not uncommon for us to look at a passage or parable in Scripture side on, as if we are somehow removed from it, claiming comradeship with the better, more praiseworthy side. In the well-known parable of the prodigal son, for example, we would see this ungrateful son rebelliously receding into the middle distance while we remain the wiser, more knowing son, looking on.

But if we believe that Scripture best interprets Scripture, then "all we like sheep have gone astray" (Isa 53:6) and so have all been in that lost son's shoes, some for many years (me, for nearly 29). If we apply that parable to a life post conversion, it bespeaks our tendency to put too much emphasis on material, physical blessings at the expense of spiritual, eternal truths which alone can satisfy the soul. We may well have been graciously granted "the best robe" of justification, the "ring" of glorification, and shoes of sanctification (Luke 15:22), but we still need to be washed regularly, for "He that is washed needeth not save to wash *his* feet, but is clean every whit" (John 13:10).

The redeemed prodigal, ie. all who have been saved, must remember the need for daily repentance and Father-ward faith. We need to be especially wary of the temptations peculiar to religion; one-third of the parable is about the lack of grace displayed by the elder son rather than wayward and foolishly straying younger son. "Angry" (Luke 15:28) at his Father's work in the life of a worthless sinner, resentful at the perceived lack of outward blessings for the years he had served, proud at not having outwardly "transgressed . . . at any time thy commandment" (v. 29), unlike others.

In some ways this parable could be called the parable of the lost and found. When we were lost we might have been tempted to fear descending "into the deep" (Rom 10:7) of despair; when we were found we might have become tempted to minimize grace, insidiously believing in our own righteousness, as if this could somehow improve our pathway "into heaven" (Rom 10:6). Both unwise extremes are addressed; it is a relief to remember that Christ Jesus, the "appointed heir of all things" (Heb 1:2), graciously did for us what we could never do through meritorious works: "For by one offering he hath perfected for ever them that are sanctified" (Heb 10:14). Thus assured, we may seek more heartily the gracious gathering in of our long-lost brethren.

Verses referred to

Isaiah 53:6

Luke 15:22, 28—29

John 13:10

Romans 10:6—7

Hebrews 1:2, 10:14

O prodigal

O prodigal, the Father knew
how much He'd set His love on you,
for even when you'd barely turned
He placed His finest robe on you.

O prodigal, the Father saw
how far you'd gone with pig and boar,
you'd scarcely in your heart returned,
He gave His ring, your conscience raw.

O prodigal, the Father cared
how you would cope when fangs were bared,
you'd hardly taken any step,
He shod your feet with shoes prepared.

O prodigal, the Father planned
how you'd be drawn to holy land,
and even now, before the feast
your best Brother shows you His hand.

Perseverance of the saints 3

In the Book of Esther we see the perseverance of the more mature saint Mordecai as he "rent his clothes . . . and went out into the midst of the city" (Esth 4:1), alongside the less experienced saint Esther as she prepared to risk her life, going "in unto the king, which *is* not according to the law" (v.16). They could so easily have preserved their own earthly comforts and benefits, but like Moses spurned the easy enjoyments of this world for the far greater glory of our Father's heavenly kingdom.

Meanwhile, the pride and fury of Haman is relentless, intense and specifically targeted. His rage is almost uncontrollable, being "full of wrath" (Esth 3:5), "full of indignation" (5:9) and full of "the glory of his riches" (v.11). We ought not forget that Satan is actively and persistently "the accuser of our brethren" (Rev 12:10), with "great wrath, because he knoweth that he hath but a short time" (v.12).

Whether through religious or political leaders, Satan manifests himself in a variety of guises, perhaps the most subtle and insidious being through certain celebrated preachers whose public words seemingly uphold the biblical doctrine of faith in Christ, but who are in fact "false apostles, deceitful workers, transforming themselves into the apostles of Christ" (2 Cor 11:13). As shocking as it sounds, it should be "no marvel; for Satan himself is transformed into an angel of light" (v.14).

Whether in (Mordecai and Esther's) eventual prosperity, or in (Job or Jonah's) sudden adversity, Satan will never leave us alone and especially targets us in times of change or uncertainty, when godly habits and routines might in some way be being threatened or disrupted.

May we struggle for the glory and glory in the struggle, being assured that our trials of prosperity and adversity are "for *our* profit, that *we* might be partakers of his holiness" (Heb 12:10), knowing that our hate-filled, pride-filled, age-old accuser shall one day be "cast into the lake of fire and brimstone, where the beast and the false prophet *are*, and shall be tormented day and night for ever and ever" (Rev 20:10).

Verses referred to

Esther 3:5, 4:1, 16, 5:9, 11   Hebrews 12:10

2 Corinthians 11:13—14   Revelation 12:10, 12, 20:10

Look!

When tired, in turmoil, or transition
Satan gets into position,
roaring leonine ambition
thwarting grace his only mission.

Through fatigue, flux, or frustration
Satan moves as is his station,
once near God, now no relation
sin's his rule, retaliation.

Change or charm or challenge comes
Satan is there, hear how he hums,
first sinful depths, expertly plumbs
then souls for scrap, he does his sums.

By hook or crook or by the book
Satan's the bait Christ never took,
for all of us before mistook
Satan for Christ, saved sinners, look!

Sola scriptura 4

Ours is an instant global culture which seems to be manifesting increasing hatred, fury, scorn, and persecution of any who dare to represent and articulate the heritage and possibilities of the Gospel. In nearly all arenas of modern life there seems to be antipathy towards foundational propositions, a real hatred of exposing or examining basic philosophical assumptions. The Word of Truth, however, is soul saving and is why "... Paul, as his manner was, went in unto them, and three sabbath days reasoned with them out of the scriptures" (Acts 17:2). His agenda in his day as ours should be in ours, was not just academic but was full of pathos: "Now while Paul waited for them at Athens, his spirit was stirred in him, when he saw the city wholly given to idolatry" (v.16).

Vested interests, deep prejudices, financial survival, career kudos etc. hold sway in the minds of most, thus "the Jews which believed not, moved with envy" (v.5) as Paul threatened their cherished status, credibility, and rectitude, foreshadowing a spiritual battle which has reverberated in many state-sponsored oppressively inclusive churches down the ages. The Jews of Thessalonica were the noble exceptions "in that they received the word with all readiness of mind, and searched the scriptures daily, whether those things were so" (v.11). How few in our day seem to be hungering for righteousness, holding preachers and teachers to account, doing a personal litmus test of Scriptural verification rather than blindly relying on favored personalities.

Paul in Acts 19 is seen not as an antagonist to truth but an existential threat to the craftsmen who were peddling their wares based on the cult of Diana: "Sirs, ye know that by this craft we have our wealth" (v.25). Similarly, in a modern Western setting one can only imagine the reaction if a faithful, fearless preacher of the Gospel were to start preaching Christ in a state-school assembly, political debate, or popular evening television chat show; the whole city likewise would be "filled with confusion" (v.29), steps would be taken to ban such hate speech, so-called, from occurring again, because their "craft is in danger to be set at nought" (v.27), their credibility exposed as mere assertion.

Paul in Acts 22 lay bare his soul and witnessed both to his impeccable credentials as a Jew and unsought conversion through Jesus Christ. However, he was met not with soul searching or Scriptural consideration but blood hatred in the form of death threats: "And they gave him audience unto this word, and *then* lifted up their voices, and said, Away with such a *fellow* from the earth: for it is not fit that he should live" (v. 22). There are many countries in our age in which there is little to no respect for human rights, where one can be put to death for daring to depart from the state religion or ideology. Along with Paul, may we champion the Bible alone, "believing all things which are written in the law and in the prophets" (Acts 24:14), seeking to "have always a conscience void of offence toward God, and *toward* men" (v.16).

Verses referred to

Acts 17:2, 5, 11, 16, 19:25, 27, 29, 22:22, 24:14, 16

The Light

This whole world is based on falsehood
shrouded as we are in selfhood,
living life without despair
each day as though death were not there.

This vain planet calls each good
not seeing that not one is good,
for if we felt that God were there
we'd crash this system—devil's lair.

This old sphere does chase its tail
calling the Bible's truth a tale,
creating rules for every right
none seeing that no soul is right.

This young ball is moving braille
only the chosen grasp its grail,
oh burdened soul, saved by the Light
only in Jesus are you light.

Sola fide 4

There are many ups and downs in the life of the believer, and yet "whom the Lord loveth he chasteneth, and scourgeth every son whom he receiveth" (Heb 12:6). We see, then, in the lives of Saul vs. David how one was left alone in order to expose the false nature of his unregenerate heart; the other disciplined and chastised so as to reveal the true, regenerated nature of his godly heart. Saul like Judas a millenium later, was led to a place of despair, whereas David like Peter to a place of greater fruitfulness and faith.

As the heart grows either colder or warmer, it becomes evident who is running "with patience the race that is set before us" (Heb 12:1), and who is not. But how can we, who are deeply disappointing, trust our hearts? It is only as we look "unto Jesus the author and finisher of *our* faith" (Heb 12:2). If we find ourselves growing cold, disobedient, fearful of the darkness within, how can we not turn *from* these things and *to* the Light, trusting in the glory of another, the Author who has not yet perfected us?

In today's terms, Saul like a modern-day mega-church televangelist had it all; "a choice young man . . . higher than any of the people" (1 Sam 9:2). Yet in eternal terms he was lifeless, "dead in trespasses and sins" (Eph 2:1), persecuting David without cause, turning to a witch rather than the Lord, ultimately ending his own life through fear of what man might do to him (1 Sam 31:4). David, on the other hand, was someone who loved and trusted the Lord, through ups and downs finding himself in Him, by faith.

May we increasingly "lay aside every weight, and the sin which doth so easily beset *us*" (Heb 12:1), that we might honor the Lord of glory through saving faith.

Verses referred to

1 Samuel 9:2, 31:4

Ephesians 2:1

Hebrews 12:1—2, 6

God's Goliath

David trusted in the Lord,
and by God's people was adored.
Saul saw David as Goliath,
not a stone from God to trieth.

David panted for God's face,
with Christ in view he grew in grace.
Saul though king of Israel,
deep in his heart was growing frail.

David ran and saw for miles,
he took God's tests, endured His trials.
Saul accepted not God's plan,
and so was less and less God's man.

David killed not God's anointed,
fearing all that's God appointed.
Saul tried to preserve his seed
(he should have cried to see his need!)

Sola gratia 4

A Christian with Arminian leanings might want to emphasize that sense of Moses choosing: "And Moses said, I will now turn aside" (Exod 3:3), but the preceding verse shows no hint of Moses doing anything other than responding, the Lord first starting to prepare him: "And the angel of the LORD appeared unto him" (Exod 3:2); the pre-incarnate Lord Jesus first appears to Moses; no mention is made of Moses choosing or seeking Him. "The bush *was* not consumed" points to the ultimate crucifixion and resurrection of this uncreated Son of God, who though divine would go on to dwell in an actual human body, therein to withstand an eternity of punishment for multitudes.

The Lord deals in such a gracious and fatherly way to Moses as Moses' initial reluctance and weakness tests His parental patience: "And the anger of the LORD was kindled against Moses" (Exod 4:14). However, Moses is soon convicted of his foolishness and like the initially reluctant son in the parable, "He answered and said, I will not: but afterward he repented, and went" (Matt 21:29).

Half a millennium later, the people of God would cry out "quicken us, and we will call upon thy name. Turn us again, O LORD God of hosts, cause thy face to shine; and we shall be saved" (Ps 80:18-19). Three millennia later we are reminded of our inability to turn ourselves to the Lord, even after many years of believing: "as for me, my feet were almost gone; my steps had well nigh slipped" (Ps 73:2). Yet it is in these moments when we are in the "backside of the desert" (Exod 3:1) of our affliction, difficulty, or temptation that the Lord will appear and call us again.

By grace not human merit we are led again to "follow him: for" by faith we "know his voice" (John 10:4), not in a mystical sense but as it is, burning in His word.

Verses referred to

Exodus 3:1—3, 4:14   Matthew 21:29

Psalm 73:2 80:18-19   John 10:4

Night as day

How can I capture in my verse
the God of all the universe,
and yet He spoke through earthern men
each one entrusted as His pen.

How can I capture in my rhyme
the God outside of space and time,
and yet He wrote on every heart
His law from which we all depart.

How can I capture in my words
the God who made beasts, fish and birds,
and yet He dwells in each conscience
our struggle quells not His patience.

How can I capture in this ink
the God without whom none can think,
and yet He draws us thus to pray
in Christ as perfect, night as day.

Solo Christo 4

There is a tendency within us either to worship or demonize the creature at the drop of a hat. The people of Melita, for example, labelled Paul a "murderer" (Act 28:4) due to his being attacked by a snake, only to label him a "god" a few verses later (v.6)! Similarly, "multitudes" (Matt 11:7) were quick to label John the Baptist and the Lord Jesus demon-possessed (v. 18), "gluttonous", a "winebibber", and sinful (v.19). In the same chapter the Holy One whom all should have worshipped, graciously commands lost souls to "Come unto me" (v.28), "Take my yoke upon you, and learn of me" (v.29).

People are so ready and willing to worship in ways which effectively allow them to dwell in sinful self-indulgence and irresponsibility: Aliens, the Multiverse, AI, Atheism, Eastern mysticism, Utopianism, Hedonism, Science Fiction, movies, games, sports, books, narratives, and a plethora of other novelties capturing and fueling our ungodly imaginations. Meanwhile, the "man of sorrows" makes us uncomfortable, squeamish, embarrassed to say the least. As we "despised" and "esteemed him not" (Isa 53:3), so do we, have we, will we . . . always. It is the hidden principle of sin within us, which will go on forever if not broken and re-set.

Or we say we are Christian but worship a dead Jesus, a distant, unknowable one who bears no resemblance to the Jesus of Scripture. The woman of Samaria, for instance, was amazed not only at the identity of the Messiah, "I that speak unto thee am *he*", but that such a one as He should deign to speak with such a one as her: "Jesus saith unto her" (John 4:26). Well, reader, you and I are one with this unworthy recipient of grace. Not a single one of us can be said to be worthy of His presence, godly care, sanctifying operation. May it be that as Christ is "the light" (John 8:12) so God will say "Let there be light" (Gen 1:3) in the darkness of you.

Verses referred to

Genesis 1:3

Isaiah 53:3

Matthew 11:7, 18—19, 28—29

John 4:26, 8:12

Acts 28:4, 6

The death of sin

Not what He looked like that did count
but only Him, His life did count,
He was the first-born from the dead
He is the church, the body's Head.

Not what He taught that showed the way
but He Himself, He is the way,
our prayers and thoughts rely on Him
our Father's light filters through Him.

Not just His actions qualified
but that it was Him, He has died,
for none created could have paid
for all created He has made.

Not what He bore outwardly shows
that suffering, none of us knows,
the pain of sin, His agony
the death of sin for you and me.

Soli Deo Gloria 4

A.W Pink's classic, *The Attributes of God*, starts with the *The Solitariness of God*, an attribute seldom touched upon by preachers. As Pink puts it: "God was under no constraint, no obligation, no necessity to create. That He chose to do so was purely a sovereign act on His part, caused by nothing outside Himself, determined by nothing but His own mere good pleasure; for He 'worketh all things after the counsel of His own will' (Eph. 1:11). That He did create was simply for His manifestative glory."

Before our modern, media-driven minds begin to buckle, let us follow a little further: "There was a time, if 'time' it could be called, when God, in the unity of His nature (though subsisting equally in three Divine Persons), dwelt all alone. 'In the beginning, God.' There was no heaven, where His glory is now particularly manifested. There was no earth to engage His attention. There were no angels to hymn His praises; no universe to be upheld by the word of His power. There was nothing, no one, but God; and that, not for a day, a year, or an age, but 'from everlasting.'"

Manwardly, Christ Jesus is the "Alpha and Omega, the beginning and the ending . . . which is, and which was, and which is to come, the Almighty" (Rev 1:8). Godwardly, the Almighty has always ever been, eternally, dwelling in perfect Triunity, devoid of such creaturely characteristics as need, loneliness, regret: "And now, O Father, glorify thou me with thine own self with the glory which I had with thee before the world was" (John 17:5).

It ought to fill us with a gradually expanding sense of wonder and ponderment that, while we rightly revere the holy word of God, God is infinitely, eternally greater than His word. Frankly, it is impossible to meditate upon this for too long in our present mortal state. What a day it will be when it won't.

Verses referred to

John 17:5

Ephesians 1:11

Revelation 1:8

True life story

Oh you have sinned when not yet out of bed
by holding not God's glory in your head,
and your whole day rests on what next you do,
repent, put on God's armor made for you.

Oh go not far in thought or word or deed
without beholding Christ, the promised seed,
He cannot bless your sin or compromise
He knows you from your prayers, not from your eyes.

Oh think upon the holiness of God
no thought of man can do justice to God,
if mortal eyes cannot behold the sun
how much more hallowed He who made the sun.

Oh step into the world so drenched in prayer
that you will not so often stumble, stare,
but think on Christ, the only true life story
hating that within which clouds His fulgent glory.

Total depravity 4

It is neither the materially poor nor the materially rich whom the Bible calls blessed, but the spiritually poor: "Blessed *are* the poor in spirit: for theirs is the kingdom of heaven" (Matt 5:3). To be "poor in spirit" means first to begin to realize one's inability to give anything to God. There is nothing we might think, say, or do that isn't tainted with our original sin-nature inherited from Adam; we have nothing to give and so we hold out our hands in helpless supplication. Even this supplication isn't giving anything to God but showing that no strength or righteousness dwells within.

Second, to be "poor in spirit" means to realize that our account stands not merely at zero; we are not merely neutral or null and void but hideously indebted by an exorbitant amount that defies calculation. Even by the time we are a young person the number of thoughts, words, and deeds which have violated God's moral law and been debited from our account constitutes an iceberg in the soul, weighing us down and taking us far from Him. This status is alarming; at some point it starts to trouble those and those alone whom the Bible calls "blessed".

Third, to be "poor in spirit" means to begin to behold that most awful, spiritually towering inferno of a task which fell to our sinless Substitute, God's holy Lamb. The apostle Paul speaks for all saved souls when he confesses himself to be "less than the least of all saints" (Eph 3:8), one who can only *begin* to fathom what his blessed Sin-bearer did for him. Once we feel our spiritual poverty, we marvel with him at "the unsearchable riches of Christ" (Eph 3:8). We rejoice and yet follow the next link in that sacred eightfold chain: "Blessed *are* they that mourn: for they shall be comforted" (Matt 5:4).

The illuminating joy of our justification is too often clouded by the presence of ongoing, indwelling sins. Let us behold, therefore, that glorious, everlasting realm to come, in which "there shall be no more death, neither sorrow, nor crying" (Rev 21:4), "and the Lamb *is* the light thereof" (Rev 21:23).

Verses referred to
Matthew 5:3—4   Revelation 21:4, 23

Ephesians 3:8

That holy fountain

Oh but there's a terrible darkness
threatening my deepest parts,
a glimpse of it I sometimes get
I call on Christ and it departs.

Oh but there's abomination
waiting in the wings for me,
not often seen but sometimes felt
I cry to Him on Calvary.

Oh but there's a shocking evil
lurking there within my thoughts,
a wicked seed, all for conception
Christ is there, my sin aborts.

Oh but there's residual hatred
my own poison in my well,
again I need that holy fountain
by His blood I'm saved from hell.

Unconditional election 4

What a wonderful yet humbling thing to know one's conversion to Christ was completely outside of oneself. No credit, originating power, or human glory could or can be associated with it, for it was determined before time began, before man or 'Adam' was created from the dust. If the salvation of a soul could even be 0.1% attributable to one particle of human merit then the palace of sovereign election would crumble, for the glory of the Creator would have to be shared with another.

So thankful we are that we remain 100% dependent on the Lord, not just for conversion but for preservation and lifelong guidance, for "O LORD, I know that the way of man *is* not in himself: *it is* not in man that walketh to direct his steps" (Jer 10:23). It is not just that the way of man is different to the way of God, it is that the way of man is not *in* himself at all; in no man is there any spiritual advancement, any way, any truth, any life outside of Christ.

Not only this, but our footsteps are directionless, thought processes broken, minds far from God's thoughts. Once a believer is raised from the ground of unbelief, it is God who directs his steps. That is not to say that we always obey, or that He puts us upon a conveyor-belt from which there is no possibility of deviation. Far from it, as we can see in the lives of God's children from Genesis Adam to Revelation John, and beyond into the gospel age. However, it is not *in* man to self-sanctify or self-bless or engage in DIY Christianity, as if all the conditions we need to meet are found within. Such a concept is alien to faith—faith looks without, to Christ.

There is nothing *in* oneself; the world is wrong when it tells you there is; Eastern mysticism is wrong when it tells you you can escape the self. The key is not to find yourself or lose yourself but to find yourself in the eternal I AM, the only ocean into which you may be truly submerged and fulfilled. The key is to spurn a life lived as an empty shell upon a fading shore, instead being "found in him" (Phil 3:9), being reckoned "dead indeed unto sin, but alive unto God through Jesus Christ our Lord" (Rom 6:11).

Verses referred to

Jeremiah 10:23   Philippians 3:9
Romans 6:11

the One

I didn't choose my birth
and I will never choose my death
so how on earth while here on earth
can I receive a new-born's breath?

I didn't choose to live again
but Jesus called me from the dead,
but now I'm here I'm born again
I know it as I know my head.

You look the same if you ask me
you are yourself, you cannot choose,
you're Lazarus as I am me,
I'm Nicodemus, head of Jews.

You are but wrapped up in yourself
as I was wrapped up in graveclothes,
you will receive a new-born self
when you believe no more in oaths.

This Nazarene, this man Jesus,
I met him once, a one to one,
but tell me this much Lazarus,
do you believe he is the One?

This Nazarene is the Messiah,
God has come in fleshly form,
the Holy One of Psalms, Isaiah,
entering to earth transform.

So you say and so he says
but many think it's heresy,
I see foul sinners on him gaze
and think on holy prophecy.

So you think and so we stink,
there is none righteous, no not one,
He is our righteousness, our link,
His blood will mean God's will is done.

Limited atonement 4

It is a reasonable thing for a believer to be asked, *When did you first believe?* or *When were you saved?* To this question might come the response *In such and such a year*, referring to that time when the "day star" (2 Pet 1:19) first arose in your heart and your lost soul went "from darkness to light" (Acts 26:18).

But the point of origination, soul's anchor, goes far deeper; further than the "given" (John 6:65) impulse of coming to the risen Savior and falling before His feet; back before the pages of the New Testament and Abrahamic covenant ("And I will establish my covenant between me and thee and thy seed" Gen 17:7); further than the ancient Fall of Man and subsequent prophecy ("between thy seed and her seed" Gen 3:15); beyond the first Creation in which the One through whom all things were made knew that as "the Lamb" He would in time be "slain from the foundation of the world" (Rev 13:8).

It finds itself in a realm which defies all human comprehension and imagination, where time as we know it ceases to be; to a holy, immutable purpose solemnly originating *within* the Godhead: "Father, I will that they also, whom thou hast given me, be with me where I am; that they may behold my glory, which thou hast given me: for thou lovedst me before the foundation of the world" (John 17:24). If I find myself loving God and trusting in Him, I give thanks and praise unto Him, knowing that it was all of Him. I would have gone an entirely different way were it not for His sovereign dealings with me, through Christ.

How we pray that we may be of the *they* (of John 17:24), not resting precariously upon a mere human decision or personal choice or dramatic conversion, but upon God the Son: "For other foundation can no man lay than that is laid, which is Jesus Christ" (1 Cor 3:11). Let Him limit you who (from our limited perspective) limited Himself in His incarnation, His atoning death, His glorious resurrection; settled in eternity, set in time, setting in eternity.

Verses referred to

Genesis 3:15, 17:7

John 6:65, 17:24

Acts 26:18

1 Corinthians 3:11

2 Peter 1:19

Revelation 13:8

Eden, Adam, Israel

What foolishness, natural selection
when you know divine election,
Eden, Adam, Israel
chosen by God, allowed to fail.

What oxymoron, self-made man
when you can see God's holy plan,
as if the world's our copyright
and not the Lord's in every right.

What wickedness, what false escape
to say that man is but an ape,
our consciences, our intellects
our souls God given, He collects.

What fools we are for money–time
entangled in this pantomime,
and yet the Door is open still
Christ is the cure, self is the ill.

Irresistible grace 4

While there would seem to be an element of choice in Ruth's cleaving to godly old Naomi, the reality is that she was irresistibly drawn by grace to choose Naomi's path. Orpah "kissed" Naomi (Ruth 1:14), using her worldly-minded common sense to take the advice given to her, advice which in Ruth's case was overruled for her eternal good. However, that seeking heart and trusting mind had been bestowed by God in the first place; madness to claim otherwise: "For who maketh thee to differ *from another*? and what hast thou that thou didst not receive? now if thou didst receive *it*, why dost thou glory, as if thou hadst not received *it*?" (1 Cor 4:7).

The chain of events which then occurred from Ruth's human perspective, were no doubt filled with prayerful waiting, emotional trembling, mental trusting, physical walking by faith, uncertain exactly how things would pan out—rolling her cares upon the promised Seed. The Bible accommodates itself to our human perspective: "and her hap was to light on a part of the field *belonging* unto Boaz" (Ruth 2:3); and then "Boaz came" (2:4), "Boaz answered" (2:11), "Boaz commanded" (2:15). Ruth then "came softly, and uncovered his feet, and laid her down" (3:7), as if any of these providential events were ever in doubt and not ordained before time was founded by our heavenly Father. He even overruled the heart of Ruth's nearest kinsman: "And he said, I will redeem *it*" (4:4), "for I cannot redeem *it*" (4:6), tying himself up in worldly-minded nonsense.

Thus, nothing in this life of ours is left to chance because chance does not exist, every "sparrow" being known of God, as "the very hairs of your head are all numbered" (Matt 10:29, 30). What then with those notions of human achievement, personal genius, sovereignty of reason? Into the gutter with them, while the golden thread of His story slowly but surely threads human souls through the Holy One, in whom Ruth's life was graciously ordained to be entwined:

> "Abraham begat Isaac;
> and Isaac begat Jacob;
> and Jacob begat Judas and his brethren;

and Judas begat Phares and Zara of Thamar;

and Phares begat Esrom;

and Esrom begat Aram;

and Aram begat Aminadab;

and Aminadab begat Naasson;

and Naasson begat Salmon;

and Salmon begat Booz of Rachab;

AND BOOZ BEGAT OBED OF RUTH;

and Obed begat Jesse;

and Jesse begat David the king;

and David the king begat Solomon of her *that had been the wife* of Urias;

and Solomon begat Roboam;

and Roboam begat Abia;

and Abia begat Asa;

and Asa begat Josaphat;

and Josaphat begat Joram;

and Joram begat Ozias;

and Ozias begat Joatham;

and Joatham begat Achaz;

and Achaz begat Ezekias;

and Ezekias begat Manasses;

and Manasses begat Amon;

and Amon begat Josias;

and Josias begat Jechonias and his brethren, about the time they were carried away to Babylon:

and after they were brought to Babylon, Jechonias begat Salathiel;

and Salathiel begat Zorobabel;

and Zorobabel begat Abiud;

and Abiud begat Eliakim; and Eliakim begat Azor;

and Azor begat Sadoc;

and Sadoc begat Achim;

and Achim begat Eliud;

and Eliud begat Eleazar;

and Eleazar begat Matthan;

and Matthan begat Jacob;

and Jacob begat Joseph the husband of Mary,
of whom was born <u>JESUS, WHO IS CALLED CHRIST</u>" (Matt 1:2–16).

Verses referred to

Ruth 1:14, 2:3—4, 11, 15, 3:7, 4:4, 6

Matthew 1:2–16, 10:29—30

1 Corinthians 4:7

One among us

As every seed hath not a claim
until the sun draws out its need,
we grow up self-content in frame,
until the Son exposes need.

So Ruth did labor in the field,
expecting nothing for her time,
till Boaz wondered, then did yield,
in God Almighty's perfect time.

For every plant there is a plan,
a blueprint made before the stars,
some go to seed, some reach their span,
some turn to God, some worship stars.

As Ruth obeyed old Naomi,
Boaz obeyed eternal God,
defying all astronomy,
Ruth's womb would bear a womb for God.

So every tree of life among us
inwardly hath streams of tears,
behold the holy One among us,
crucified and scorned with jeers!

Perseverance of the saints 4

There is so much rich application to be drawn out of those two believers believers' walk to Emmaus, that it is hard to pen just a few paragraphs. Following hot on the heels of a faithless response to the news of the Resurrection ("And their words seemed to them as idle tales, and they believed them not" Luke 24:11), we are introduced to Cleopas and another unnamed disciple, his anonymity serving to enable us to identify with and insert ourselves into his shoes. The two "talked together of all these things which had happened" (v. 14), then "communed *together* and reasoned" (v. 15). Perhaps like believers of today they lamented the sorry state of society, the foolishness of rulers, the hypocrisy of the religious leaders who should have known better. They may have discussed the future of the church, the unfolding of God's providence, the relative attributes of the brethren in Christ, and many other things. However, they missed one thing and it turned out to be that which they ought to have strained every brain cell and nerve ending to apprehend—conscious communion with the Lord Jesus Christ.

In that same verse we learn that "Jesus himself drew near, and went with them" (v.15). Like us, they were genuine believers sought out by God, yet so preoccupied as to miss the unspeakable blessing in their midst, so close and amenable. What a message to believers in all subsequent centuries. We may pray, read our Bibles, attend church, teach Sunday school, preach sermons, engage in all manner of evangelistic and ecclesiastical endeavors, yet miss Christ!

It is not that we are hypocrites or apostates or even backsliders; more a question of prioritizing and consciously focusing upon the one thing needful: "For I determined not to know any thing among you, save Jesus Christ, and him crucified" (1 Cor 2:2). If we do anything spiritually: engaging in apologetics, exegesis, doctrine, conferences, ministries, outreach, or other good deeds etc. let us get to Christ, just as all proverbial roads lead to Rome, all preservation to the Ark of Noah, all pathways to the City of Refuge.

The Lord Jesus then conducted the mother of all Bible studies: "And beginning at Moses and all the prophets, he expounded unto them in all the scriptures the things concerning himself" (Luke 24:27). Whether in the book of Leviticus, Ezekiel, Jonah or Haggai, Christ is there and should always be being actively sought. There are multitudes of applications and relevant doctrines which may apply to the issues of our day, all of which are important and have their place. But if we miss Christ or don't end up getting to and giving Him the glory then how much duller our hearts, how sinfully downcast and disconcerted we can become. May every Christian sermon, service, conversation, fellowship meeting, meal, or outing be filled with the primacy of the all-conquering Christ:

"And they said one to another, Did not our heart burn within us, while he talked with us by the way, and while he opened to us the scriptures?" (v.32).

Only then will all other things find their rightful place.

Verses referred to

Luke 24:11, 14—15, 27, 32

1 Corinthians 2:2

Sea Song

In oceanic bliss I sank
stealing my body, plummeting,
while all around me drowning souls
not one defying gravity.

No one to turn to, none to thank
no rock of rest on which to rest,
while all around me blinded shoals
not one not in depravity.

And then upon my back I felt
a warmth, a light, not of the sea,
the salt began to sting my eyes
I lifted as was lifted up.

The land beneath my toes was felt
though soaked, at once I now could see
my Savior moved me, heard my cries
He drowned my ocean in His cup.

And so my journey did begin
my clothes now dry, now wet again,
my battle is to dry my sin
as Christ subsumed it with His pain.

Some days I feel I'm almost dry
and then the quicksand's at my feet
I'm sinking in an inward sty
until I see my Savior's feet.